Small Town
Big Dreams

by
Tom Ward

Churchill Press
ChurchillPress.org

Small Town Big Dreams
Copyright 2019 by Tom Ward

First Edition

Dedication

For Elizabeth, Mary Frances,
Thomas, and Sarah Margaret.

Gratitude

Thanks to the Bainbridge family, and yes it is indeed a family, for their support, comments, and passion that have made this book a joy to compose.

Thanks to Coach Jeff Littleton, who embraced a vision for this book to celebrate the team. As always, he diverted praise toward his players and coaching colleagues. They say that a team reflects the personality of its head coach, and the championship bears proof of exactly that.

Thanks to Kristi Littleton for everything you did to help launch this project, which is probably even more than you might realize.

Thanks to the Touchdown Club, for adding both content and perspective to this book. Your assertive support and care for the players stands as a shining example for booster groups across America.

Thanks to Coach Randy and Margie Hill, for your help with the book, your perspective, and for being people whom I have admired for my entire life.

Thanks to Brian and Liz Hill, for your enormous contributions to this book. To Brian, thanks for interview time and behind-the-scenes recollections. For Liz, thanks for lending your considerable expertise as a photographer to this project and making it better.

Thanks to Roy Mathews, principal of Bainbridge High School, for your support of this book. Your understanding of leadership, education, and football have added greatly to this project.

Thanks to Jimmy Harris and Scott Miller, the athletic directors of Bainbridge High School, for your outstanding leadership of this program, especially during the stormy times of 2018. Athletic success in multiple sports starts at the top.

Thanks to Coach Chip Ariail, thanks for adding your expertise as an outstanding resource on the rich history of the Bainbridge program. Having written about sports for many years, I can confidently say that you are the best statistician with whom I've ever worked.

Thanks to Powell Cobb of *The Post Searchlight* for your adding to this book with the stories of the storm and team from the eyes of an experienced journalist. You represent a newspaper that, like the team itself, stands as a symbol of excellence far beyond the borders of Decatur County.

Thanks to Gary and Betty Ward, for time as a sounding board, for discerning reviews, and the first suggestion of writing a book about a great football town and its team.

Contents

The Staff

Jeff Littleton
Head Coach
Brian Hill
Co-Def Coord.-DB
Joe Dollar
Co-Def Coord.-OLB
Mike Harville
Offensive Coordinator-QB
Tom Wheeler
Tight Ends-OL
Larry Cosby
Running Backs
Ryan Kineard
Offensive Line
Brian McCorkle
Defensive Line
Randy Hill
Cornerbacks
Blake Cecil
Defensive Ends
Justin Palmer
9th grade head coach
Harold Smith
Sideline

Chip Ariail
Statistician
TaZion Hines
Manager
Tim Cochran
Superintendant
PJ Davis
Linebackers
Latavious Davis
9th grade def line
Daniel Forman
9th-WR
Ty Levens
Manager
Jimmy Harris
Athletic Director
Scott Miller
Athletic Director
Jonathan Anthony
Athletic Trainer
Rohan Gaines
9th grade def backs

The Team

1	Quayde Hawkins	QB	So.	6-0	160	
2	Zion Bouie	RB, DB	Fr.	5-6	150	
3	Deyon Bouie	QB, CB	Fr.	5-11	165	
4	Rashad Broadnax	RB, SS	So.	5-8	165	
5	Caleb McDowell	DB, RB, ATH	So.	5-10	170	
6	Jaylan Peterson	WR, CB	Jr.	5-9	145	
7	Aaron Spivie	WR, CB	Sr.	5-7	141	
8	Michael Ryan	WR, CB	Jr.	6-0	170	
9	Coryn Burns	SS, WR	Sr.			
10	Jaheim Jenkins	WR, QB, DB	Jr.			
11	Isaac Backey	WR, OLB	Sr.	5-8	153	
12	Courtney Thomas	OLB, FS	So.	5-7	160	
13	Braxton Johnson	WR, CB	Fr.	5-10	150	
14	Jackson Wheeler	QB, TE, DE	Jr.	6-2	227	
15	Ray Dodson	QB	Fr.	5-10	150	
16	J'von Lee	RB, LB	So.			
17	Zaccheaus Chrispen	RB, LB	Fr.	5-10	159	
18	Adrian Cooper	WR, CB	Sr.	5-11	165	
18	Jackson McCullough	TE, DE	So.			
19	Tevin Mccray	RB, SS	Jr.			
20	Lathan Levens	QB, LB	Fr.			
21	Fred Thompson	CB, WR	Sr.	5-9	155	
22	Bryce Worthy	WR, OLB	Sr.	5-11	181	
23	Ralph Register	RB, OLB	Sr.	5-10	170	
24	Tim Allison	TE, DL	Sr.	5-10	200	
25	Caleb Lewis	RB, DB	So.			
26	Anthony Brooks	LB, WR	Sr.	5-10	200	
27	Latrevian Colbert	RB	Fr.			
28	Randy Bradwell	WR, DB	Jr.			
30	Roman Harrison	DE, MLB	Sr.	6-2	232	
31	Caleb Harris	K	Sr.			
32	Jarvis Martin	MLB, FB	Jr.	5-6	170	
33	Ridge Baggett	FB, LB	So.	6-1	200	
34	Randy Fillingame	OLB, FB	Sr.	5-8	185	
35	Amari Peterson	OLB, WR	Jr.	5-10	155	
36	Sam Boutwell	OLB, DB	Jr.			
37	Eric Sanders jr.	MLB, FB	So.	5-11	187	
38	Garrett Sigman	K	Jr.			

The Team (Continued)

No.	Name	Position	Class	Height	Weight
39	Raquan Freeman	OLB, WR	So.		
40	Daylon Cosby	WR, CB	So.	5-8	148
41	Bruce Gadson	WR, OLB	Jr.	5-8	152
42	Jamorris Cosby	WR, DB	So.		
43	Nolan Barr	WR, DB	So.		
44	Bowen Dodson	MLB, TE	Sr.	5-11	215
45	Tahari Tate	FB, DE	So.		
46	Stefon Henderson	RB, DB	Fr.	5-7	138
47	Jashon Mitchell	LB, FB	Fr.		
48	Anthony (AJ) Jones	DL	Fr.		
49	Arkeavious Marshall	TE, DE	So.		
50	Vick Wimberly	DT	Jr.	6-2	225
51	Terrell Anderson(fatback)	G, C	Sr.	5-7	250
52	Dakota Eakin	OL, DL	Fr.		
52	Lawson Chandler	T	So.		
53	Ijhal Jackson	NG	Sr.		
54	Octavious Green	OL	Fr.		
55	Jacob McLaughlin	G, C	Sr.	5-10	220
56	Hunter Moore	OL, DL	Fr.		
57	Cameron Bennett	OL, DL	So.		
58	Logan Glover	OL, DL	Fr.		
59	Ben Mitchell	C	Sr.		
60	Brad Mitchell	G	Sr.		
61	Trey Harris	DE, T	Jr.	6-4	229
62	John Shephard	OL, DL	So.		
64	WIlliam McCorkle	OL, DL	Fr.		
65	Josiah Blackmon	OL, DL	Jr.	5-11	170
66	Colby Davis	DT, T	Sr.	6-2	
67	Michael Fountain	OL, DL	Fr.		
68	Dax McNair	G	Sr.		
69	Damien Scott	DT, T	Jr.		
70	Jacobey Bouie	OL, DL	Fr.		
71	Jaylon Randall	OL, DL	So.		
72	Alvin Parker III	OL, DL	Fr.	6-2	257
73	Tyree Holmes	OL, DL	So.		
74	Conner Priest	C, DT	Jr.	5-9	220
75	Timothy Thompson	OL, DL	So.		
76	Tim Anderson	G, DE	Sr.	5-8	175
77	Amari Perkins	OL, DL	Fr.		
78	Terry Thomas	OL, DL	Fr.		
79	Aaron Hughes	OL, DL	So.		

The Team

80	Simpson Bowles	TE, DE So.			
81	Kasin Taylor	OL, DL Fr.	5-9	158	
81	Logan Berry	WR, DB Fr.			
82	Kelmari Glover	WR, DB Fr.			
84	Garrett Cox	WR, DB So.			
85	Blaze Allen	TE, DL So.	6-0	185	
86	Henry Hill	DL Fr.			
87	Michael Jackson	RB, DB Fr.			
88	Walter Baca	WR, DB So.			
88	Will Beckham	WR, SS So.			
89	Kooper Kearns	OLB, ILB Fr.	5-5	140	
90	Kendall Glover	P Jr.			
91	Mason Ard	QB, K Fr.			
92	Devontay Stepney	WR, DB Fr.			
93	Luke Emmons	WR, DB Fr.			
94	Joe Parrych	DL Sr.			
95	Jaheen Cheatem	WR, DB Jr.			
96	Cory Hall	WR, DB So.			
97	Pierce Taughton	WR, DB Fr.			
98	Andrew Ryan	K Fr.			
99	Michael Smith	WR, DB Fr.			
99	Matt Hurley	WR, DB Fr.			
	Kelmarri Glover	Fr.			
	Nicholas Kyles	FS, QB So.			
	Pierce Taunton	Fr.			
	Trey Bouie	Fr.	5-7	160	

B^{The}earcat Touchdown Club

Thankfully acknowledges

The Ultimate Hunting Experience

Thanks to Southwind Plantation for supporting the
Bainbridge High School football team and also for the
purchase of books for the Bainbridge coaches and senior players.

Prologue

Leading the way

> "The pessimist complains about the wind.
>   The optimist expects it to change.
>   The leader adjusts the sails."
>
> - -John Maxwell

October 15, 2018

Bainbridge High School
One Bearcat Drive
Bainbridge, Georgia

Jeff Littleton left his house and headed for work. In a few moments, he would assume the roles of leader, educator, counselor, and father figure. They called him "Coach," but today that seemed to be the least of his titles.

The team had plenty of problems, and he was ultimately the one they would look to. There was the losing record, and the unavoidable growing pains of a squad sporting over 60 freshmen and sophomores, but those were not the problem. Not anymore. He could only wish those were the biggest problems.

Nothing about this day would remind him of an average Monday on the job. Nor would anything normal await him when he returned to his home, where he lived with his wife Kristi, his daughters, Anna Kate and Emily, and the uninvited intruder who had crashed into their house. The intruder was the large tree that had fallen through their roof.

The day would soon bring a team meeting, which itself was not unusual. Thousands of football teams were meeting that day to evaluate their performance in the previous game and begin preparing for the next one. Like the

2

day, however, the meeting would become anything but normal.

And it was all because of Michael.

Michael wasn't some troublesome teen or misbehaving coach. Michael was the first Category 5[1] hurricane to hit the continental United States in a generation. Michael was the first major hurricane to directly smash into South Georgia in a century. Michael was actually the fourth most powerful hurricane to ever hit the continental United States.[2]

> "We talked about not making excuses because of the harsh conditions. We talked about how tough times don't last but tough people do."
>
> --Coach Jeff Littleton

The people gathered at this team meeting had become much more complicated than the players and coaches they were a week ago. Now, some were virtually homeless. Some might as well be homeless, as they lived cramped into small rooms with other family members, and with no power or running water. Some weren't even there, as they had no transportation to the school for practice. Many in the community now lived in homes that were barely habitable.[3]

Some had lost most of their clothes. Many, if not most, were unable to bathe. Most depended on the local National Guard station for drinking water. Many relied on local churches and organizations for their meals. Many made good use of the bags of ice that were available in the

1   John L. Beven II, Robbie Berg, and Andrew Hagan (April 19, 2019). "Tropical Cyclone Report: Hurricane Michael" (PDF). National Hurricane Center. NOAA. Retrieved May 1, 2019. https://www.nhc.noaa.gov/data/tcr/AL142018_Michael.pdf
2   Brett, Jennifer, How Hurricane Michael made history," *Atlanta Journal-Constitution*, October 29, 2019. https://www.ajc.com/weather/hurricanes/georgia-hurricane-michael-marks-new-kind-storm/kwck2ldHMVCe-LioHENH3WL/
3   Rev. Steve Brooks (Bainbridge team chaplain) in discussion with the author, December 4, 2019.

Bainbridge High School head coach Jeff Littleton speaks with a broadcaster after the Bearcats' state championship victory. The team, and the town, traveled a long journey of rebuilding from October 10th to December 11, the date of the championship game. (Photo courtesy of Elizabeth P. HIll).

vacant lot next door to the Home Depot, but there was a two-bag limit.[4]

As the Bainbridge High School head football coach, Littleton had maintained close contact with his assistant coaches and staff. He knew their personal situations and he made sure everyone was alright. Together, they also discussed their role with the young men who were their football players and in many ways their responsibility.

Littleton and his staff had also contacted as many players as possible through their *Hudl* app. Some never got the messages because the internet was unavailable, but they connected with many of their players. "We felt, as a staff, that our kids would want to be removed from the mess that was delivered by the hurricane," Littleton explained.[5]

The team meeting began with the coaches and play-

4   Decatur County EMA - Bainbridge, GA, Facebook, October 12, 2018. https://www.facebook.com/Decatur-County-EMA-Bain-bridge-GA-1421794984594631/
5   Jeff Littleton (Bainbridge head football coach) in discussion with the author, December 3, 2019.

ers speaking frankly about the upheavals of their lives before discussing football. "We all talked about each other's
damage at our homes, and who wasn't able to make it to
practice for various reasons. Most of our kids commented
about wanting to come to practice to get away from the
cleanup."

That brought plenty of laughter.

"It wasn't a funny topic but the kids used it in a positive way to lighten the situation. That was important, because most of them had no power or any way to take a
bath. But our field house had running water, so the kids
were more interested in practice than ever before."[6]

Then it was time to lead.

The kids could see their immediate needs like power, water, and of course the internet. They could see their
need to use their smartphones and the looming need to
resume schoolwork. They could even see their football
team's upcoming battle against an undefeated opponent
with almost no time to prepare.

All of those things, even the football game, were
challenges that would come and go soon. The most important task before these young men, Littleton knew, was
dealing with adversity. Suddenly, these guys had to do
schoolwork, help clean up their damaged or destroyed
homes and show up at their football games in front of thousands of people who expected them to perform as if they
hadn't another care in the world.

"We talked about not making excuses because of
the harsh conditions," Littleton added. "We talked about
how tough times don't last but tough people do."[7]

"The players looked to Jeff and the entire staff and
then they responded in a great way," explained Randy Hill,
a retired longtime coach who still coaches the defensive
backs for Bainbridge. Hill owns no less than seven state
championship rings in two sports, so he knows something
about the formula for winning. He also understands when
players have bought in to their coach's vision and when

6   Id.
7   Id.

they have not.

"The players trusted the coaches," Hill added, "and that meant everything."[8]

Trust between players and coaches was no accident; it was a team goal from the moment that Littleton was introduced as the new head coach. In the first minute of his opening remarks to the team, he made the priority clear: "We're going to be better football players, but I want to make sure, first of all, that you become better men. We will begin to trust each other, we will care about each other, and we will love each other. We will grow together, and if we do those things, we will be better football players."[9]

The coming weeks would provide the Bainbridge High School coaches and players plenty of opportunities to either make excuses or choose to excel. Each of the Bainbridge Bearcats players would face the storm recovery, every day, as a part of their lives. In the coming weeks they would grieve even more, this time with a teammate over an irreplaceable loss.

Football might seem like an unimportant aspiration, given the circumstances. That, the coaches knew and agreed, was the entire point. Football wasn't the destination, but rather the vehicle. Football was the tool to teach these young men priceless lessons on dealing with life's inevitable challenges. Football was the tool that would teach teamwork as a source of joy rather than merely the rules of the game.

There was no school that week, so the team hung together. They practiced together. When not practicing or working at home, they came together and helped unload supplies and help with the cleanup around the community.

They might win, and they might not win, but they would do it together. As a team, they would grow stronger together.

And they would never be the same.

---

8   Randy Hill (Bainbridge defensive coach) in discussion with the author, November 21, 2019.
9   New BHS Head Football Coach Littleton Addresses the Team, YouTube video, 15:31, March 22, 2013. https://www.youtube.com/watch?v=TeD-J7G5mX_U&feature=youtu.be. Retrieved January 19, 2019.

Chapter 1

The Opening

> "There's two times of year for me: football season, and waiting for football season."
>
> --Darius Rucker

Two Months Earlier

Exam day had arrived.

For most students, an exam is a highly private event, with tests taken and submitted for the teacher's review. Grades typically remain private, and the teacher is the one who can tell who has prepared and who has chosen not to. The teacher is the only one who can recommend a different approach to interpreting a classic novel. The teacher is the only one who can explain and describe a repeated mistake in solving math problems. The exams are, rightfully so, not marked with red ink and displayed for the public.

And then there's football.

All school athletic events are public, but football is more of an event than merely a game. Like an academic exam, outstanding preparation will usually stand out. But unlike the exams in the classrooms, the public, the media, and the entire online world will have access to the results.

But even before exam day, the coaches faced their own difficult questions. Many of those involved deciding the starting lineup as opening day approached. Randy Fillingame was a rising senior, a bit undersized at 5-foot-7, but an outstanding competitor. "Having Fillingame and [Bryce] Worthy was like having extra coaches on the field," one coach recalled." Littleton and the co-defensive coordinators, Brian Hill and Joe Dollar, decided to move Fillingame to inside linebacker. It was a bit of a risk, asking a senior to switch positions, especially given his physical size.

But all position changes carry an inherent risk, swapping the known for the unknown. Fillingame, however, wasn't the only player placed somewhere other than his natural position. Roman Harrison, the Herculean defensive lineman, was a natural at defensive end or maybe the "Jack" position. On the Bainbridge team, his strength and size were needed in the middle to help stop the opponent's inside running game. The coaches also decided to play Harrison in the middle on the field goal and extra point block teams. Sooner or later, they believed, his strength and athleticism up the middle would make a difference with blocking kicks.

Even with some position changes, the defense remained solid and stood as the foundation of the team. Experienced seniors and outstanding athletes anchored the defensive side of the ball, although some younger players had the potential to break into the starting lineup.

Maybe the biggest decision of the preseason involved the most critical position in all of sports, the quarterback. The quarterbacks can't always win games, but any quarterback can lose any game to any opponent. Not only did the team lack a proven starter at quarterback, the coaches had to make a decision between three candidates for the job quickly enough to prepare the starter for the season.

The running attack would likely become the forte of the offense. Bainbridge would pound opponents with running plays, and the passing game would provide quick-strike capability for big plays. That strategy proved successful, as ultimately, eight different players would average double-figure yardage-per-catch for the season.

Paving the way for that running attack would be the offensive line. The interior of the line brought plenty of experience, with the Mitchell brothers (Ben at center and Brad at guard) and Jacob McLaughlin at the other guard. All three grew up heavily invested in the Bainbridge program. For the Mitchell brothers, their parents had each served as president of the Bearcats Touchdown Club. McLaughlin's older brother

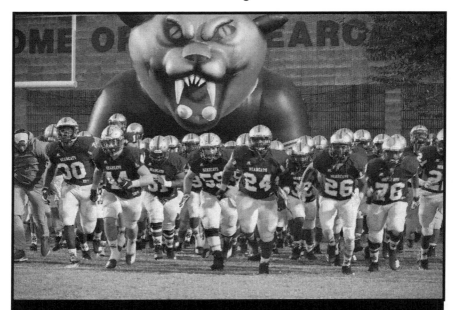

The Bainbridge Bearcats charge onto their home field before kickoff. Their performance at home was a testament to the crowd support, and their playoff road victories featured large crowds of supporters from Bainbridge who traveled to support their team.

was the starting quarterback for the 2015 Bearcats team that made it to the Class AAAAA Final Four. The playing experience was nice, but there was a problem. "Our offensive line was undersized and undermanned," explained offensive coordinator Mike Harville. "Some of our opponents outweighed us 50 to 70 pounds across the line. We really had to execute on every play."[10]

So the undersized line would determine some of the play calling. But first, the coaches had to choose the quarterback. Jackson Wheeler was a rising junior and a sizable player at 6-foot-2, 227 pounds. He also had the strongest arm and the most team experience. Wheeler was also an outstanding tight end prospect. Quayde Hawkins was a ninth-grader just a few weeks earlier, though as a rising sophomore he had one year under his belt. Hawkins brought both a strong arm and running ability, making him more of a dual-threat quarterback.

10   Joe Harville (Bainbridge offensive coach) in discussion with the author, December 14, 2019.

His wheels would help in scrambling when receivers were covered, and also with planned quarterback carries. Deyon "Smoke" Bouie brought a dynamic presence to the team, even though he was only beginning high school as a freshman. At this early stage in his high school career, Smoke was more of a running quarterback. All three, thankfully, were strong candidates for the job. No one, however, could gauge in advance how a quarterback would react in the pressure of big games, making split-second decisions with large defensive players pursuing him.

As it turned out, Smoke was not the only freshman Bouie competing for playing time as a freshman. His cousin, Zion Bouie, was also a dynamic athlete, playing defensive back. Other than quarterback, defensive back just might be the position that can most quickly lose a game for any team with a blown coverage. Placing freshmen in that role carries great risk, especially in the current era of spread offensive and more complex defensive coverages.

After a spirited competition, the coaches settled on sophomore Quayde Hawkins, the dual-threat quarterback. That gave the coaches the opportunity to place Jackson Wheeler at tight end to fortify the ground attack.

As for the Bouie cousins, having the speed and athletic ability made them potential weapons, and they would rise as high as their maturity and hard work would take them.

The year was already eight months old, and much of it had been spent preparing for this moment. On Friday, August 17, 2018, the coaches and players of the Bainbridge High School football team would take the field and end the months of waiting for another season of their hometown's favorite sport.

All the months of preparation, film study, agility drills, weightlifting, playbook study, and tackling drills would be put to a public test.

Opening day had arrived.

Across America, high school football stands alone as the sport that truly binds students, sports fans, and otherwise disparate groups of people into a community focused on the success of their youth.

They want their team to play well. They want the band to perform artfully. They want the cheerleaders to stir the crowd and provide well-choreographed routines. They want to encourage today's youth toward productive activities and achievements. They want to re-live the good things about their own high school experience.

Maybe that was why over 120,000 fans packed Chicago's Soldier Field to catch the game between Leo High School and Austin High School on November 27, 1937.[11] Or maybe that was why an Air Force flight instructor in Mississippi chose a training mission path over rural Alabama and orchestrated a Super Bowl-style flyover moments before his alma mater's playoff game kickoff to intimidate the opposing team and its fans.[12] Perhaps that same intensity inspired the McCallie board of trustees to suspend its rivalry with fellow Chattanooga prep school, Baylor, because "...losing a football game does something to you that you can't get over for weeks." And then there was the famous Cook family wedding rehearsal in the parking lot, among the tailgaters, before the Lowndes-Valdosta rivalry.[13] At least no one missed the game, and the couple was going to end up married no matter where the rehearsal was held.

Over 160 million fans[14] attend high school football games,[15] so the ritual of opening day stands tall as one of the great American traditions.

Bainbridge vs. Seminole County
August 17, 2018

The opening opponent was Seminole County, and the

11   Lynch, Thomas W, "The Big Game." Leo High School Alumni Association. https://www.leoalumni.org/the-big-game/. Retrieved January 14, 2019.
12   Anonymous U.S. Air Force officer, in discussion with the author, August, 2009, Washington, D.C.
13   WALB News 10, "Fans gear up for Valdosta and Lowndes game," October 7, 2011. https://www.walb.com/story/15644844/fans-gear-up-for-valdosta-and-lowndes-game/. Retrieved January 14, 2019.
14   Actually the number is higher, because the 165 million estimate reflects 2011 statistics, and more high schools are fielding 11-player teams than ever before.
15   Niehoff, Dr. Karissa, "The NFHS Voice: High School Football is Thriving, Not Dying," *NFHS News*, September 25, 2019. https://www.nfhs.org/articles/the-nfhs-voice-high-school-football-is-thriving-not-dying/. Retrieved November 22, 2019.

game promised to match two teams who held clear playoff potential. The Indians were looking to make their first playoff run since 2013, and all the ingredients were there. They sported a senior quarterback and plenty of experience on their roster. The question was how the Bainbridge Bearcats would match up with the Indians in this opening game, when all things remain unpredictable until the teams hit the field.

The accomplished coaching staff had prepared a thorough game plan for the game, but as the boxer Mike Tyson famously remarked: "Everybody has a plan until they get punched in the mouth."[16]

In other words, even the most artfully crafted game plans remain uncertain until the game begins.

And so it was with Seminole County. The 2018 season would become one of historic highs and lows for the Indians. They stormed off to a 4-2 start, (and 4-1 in their region),[17] ultimately making the playoffs for the first time in five years. Unfortunately, the word "storm" acquired another meaning for the Indians and their hometown of Donalsonville, just as it did for Bainbridge. After meeting for the opening game, the two schools, towns, and teams would travel similar paths to deal with the destruction of a deadly, Category 5 hurricane.

But on this night, the two playoff-bound teams hit the field, and then left it all on the field.

And on this night, the win, the stats, and all the scoring belonged to Bainbridge.

The first scoring drive of the season was only four plays, a 44-yard drive that hit pay dirt with a 15-yard run by Caleb McDowell. The extra point by Caleb Harris gave Bainbridge a quick 7-0 lead. McDowell would average almost eight yards-per-carry in the opening game.[18]

Less than two minutes later on the game clock, Indians

16   Berardino, Mike, "Mike Tyson explains one of his most famous quotes," *South Florida Sun Sentinel*, November 9, 2012. https://www.sun-sentinel.com/sports/fl-xpm-2012-11-09-sfl-mike-tyson-explains-one-of-his-most-famous-quotes-20121109-story.html. Retrieved February 20, 2019.
17   Seminole County Football Home, *maxpreps.com*, https://www.maxpreps.com/high-schools/seminole-county-indians-(donalsonville,ga)/football/home.htm
18   Game statistics provided by the Bainbridge High School Bearcats coaching staff, and specifically by statistician Chip Ariail.

quarterback Ty Moulton dropped back for a pass deep within Seminole County territory, and the result was an interception by Deyon Bouie at the 18-yard-line that was returned for a touchdown and a quick 14-0 Bainbridge lead.

The pick-six by Deyon "Smoke" Bouie set the tone for the game, as the Indians basically shut down their passing game after that. The Bainbridge defense held them without a single pass completed for the game, and less than 100 total offensive yards.

The second quarter began just as successfully for Bainbridge, with a six-play, 50-yard scoring drive. Rashad Broadnax scored on a 1-yard run, and a Garrett Sigmon extra point made the score 21-0.

Then, the rout was on.

Broadnax, who led the team with ten carries on opening night, wasn't finished scoring. With less than two minutes remaining in the first half, the Bainbridge defense had once again stopped Seminole County and forced a punt from deep in their own territory. Fielding the punt at the 46-yard-line, Broadnax exploded for a punt-return touchdown and created an insurmountable 28-0 Bainbridge lead before halftime.

The second half featured only one score, mid-way through the third quarter, with a 24-yard pass from Quayde Hawkins to Bryce Worthy to make the margin 35-0. Coach Jeff Littleton and the staff played many beyond their starters, helping younger backup players to build experience and confidence.

Overall, the game brought a dominating performance by the defense, which registered a shutout, and the offense, which performed so effectively that Bainbridge only punted one time.

Senior Coryn Burns led the stifling defense with seven tackles, while Bryce Worthy and Anthony Brooks each contributed five stops. The Bearcats registered seven tackles-for-loss. Interestingly, of their 55 tackles, almost half of them were unassisted.[19]

19   Bainbridge Schedule 2018, *MaxPreps.com*, https://www.maxpreps.com/games/8-17-2018/football-fall-18/bainbridge-vs-seminole-county.htm?c=-Jy_HMqSAg0CEmSzdEpY92A#tab=box-score&schoolid=. Retrieved July 18, 2019.

So for Seminole County, the season would bring plenty of victories and the long-awaited playoff run, but for the community of Bainbridge, their team had aced its first exam.

Bainbridge vs. Cairo
August 24, 2018

And then came Cairo.

As it turned out, 2018 was not a good year to play Cairo High School. The Syrupmakers' season would be remembered for their 10-game winning streak and a run deep into the AAAA playoffs.[20]

If you think the nickname Syrupmakers is unique, you're not alone. *Sports Illustrated* also recognized the originality of the school's nickname, placing it at the top of innovative nickname lists, alongside such classics as the Criminals, the Whoopee, the Nimrods, and the Hot Dogs.[21] ESPN named it the number-one nickname in all of high school sports.[22]

Cairo is a city defined by its names. The city was named after Cairo, Egypt,[23] but it's not pronounced like its namesake. Instead, the word is pronounced like Ka-ro. That could lead people to deduce that the Syrupmakers are named after Karo syrup, but that's just a coincidence. The nickname comes from the Roddenberry's syrup plant[24] that provided many jobs and dominated the Cairo economy for so long. As legend has it, local employees at the Roddenberry plant brought jackets to a game to keep the players dry during a storm. The jackets, bearing the name of the company, quickly gave rise to the school's nickname.

20   Cairo Football Home, *MaxPreps.com*, https://www.maxpreps.com/high-schools/cairo-syrupmakers-(cairo,ga)/football-fall-18/schedule.htm. Retrieved September 27, 2019.
21   Staples, Andy, "Ranking the nation's 15 most unique high school nicknames," *Sports Illustrated*, August 3, 2009. https://www.si.com/more-sports/2009/08/03/schools-nicknames. Retrieved April 18, 2019.
22   WXTL Tallahassee, "WTXL Road Trip: The Most Unique High School Mascot, Cairo's Syrupmakers," July 22, 2015.
https://www.wtxl.com/news/wtxl-road-trip-the-most-unique-high-school-mascot-cairo/article_0904ef9e-30ac-11e5-8589-57d42a311afb.html.
23   Id.
24   Cairo's mascot named No. 1. *TimesEnterprise.com*. https://www.timesenterprise.com/sports/cairo-s-mascot-named-no/article_25368a3d-973a-552b-9429-813e4107df15.html. Retrieved October 9, 2019.

Part of the magic of high school football is that they are events, rather than merely games. The outstanding Bainbridge High School band and majorettes entertain the crowd and show that the football players aren't the only ones who have the ability and discipline to perform at a high level on Friday nights. (Photo courtesy of Elizabeth P. Hill).

The Big Toe from Cairo became another in the city's history with names. Bobby Walden was a kicker and running back for the University of Georgia, and as the nickname reveals, he was especially talented as a kicker and punter. Walden was the punter for two Super Bowl championships with the Pittsburgh Steelers, in Super Bowl IX (over the Minnesota Vikings) and X (over the Dallas Cowboys).

And perhaps the most interesting name of them all was the one whose name was lost to history...two different times. Mack Robinson, a Cairo native and African-American, was a track star who went to the 1936 Berlin Olympic Games and broke the world record in the 200-meter run in front of Adolph Hitler himself. Nobody remembers Robinson, however, because another American, Jesse Owens, ran even faster and captured the gold medal.[25]

25   IMDB biography of Mack Robinson, https://www.imdb.com/name/

So Mack Robinson made history as a silver medalist in the Olympic Games, but wasn't even the most memorable person in his family. That distinction belonged to his little brother and fellow Cairo native, a baseball player named Jackie.[26] The name Jackie Robinson transcends sports and stands for the remarkable courage, poise and class the Brooklyn Dodgers star showed when he broke the racial barrier in Major League Baseball. Each year, in one game, all players in the sport don the number 42 on their jersey to celebrate the history of Mack Robinson's little brother.

Some of the names in Cairo's history now stood with the Bainbridge team. Coach Littleton and Coach Brian Hill served as defensive coaches on a state championship team and also the state runner-up team the year before. In his opening remarks to the team in 2013, one of the first facts Littleton made clear was that he had been a Cairo guy, but now he was a Bainbridge man.[27]

The name Cairo would appear in the win column for most of their games in 2018, but when they faced the team from Bainbridge, they were in for an old-fashioned, defensive slugfest.

The Bainbridge defense had registered a shutout against Seminole County, and the second game would not be much different. Early in the game it didn't seem that way, as a first quarter, 35-yard touchdown pass put the Syrupmakers on the board early.[28]

But that was it.

Cairo would not score again in the 15-7 Bainbridge victory. The game was clearly important, but as Cairo averaged 38 points-per-game[29] during its 10-game winning streak, the dominating performance by the Bearcats defense became

nm1862562/bio. Retrieved February 20, 2019.
26   Id.
27   New BHS Head Football Coach Littleton Addresses the Team, YouTube video, 15:31, March 22, 2013. https://www.youtube.com/watch?v=TeDJ7G-5mX_U&feature=youtu.be. Retrieved January 19, 2019.
28   Game statistics provided by the Bainbridge High School Bearcats coaching staff, and specifically by statistician Chip Ariail.
29   Cairo Football Home, MaxPreps.com, https://www.maxpreps.com/high-schools/cairo-syrupmakers-(cairo,ga)/football-fall-18/schedule.htm. Retrieved September 27, 2019.

even more impressive.

The Bainbridge defense held the Syrupmakers offense to an anemic 3-for-12 on third-down conversions and sacked the Cairo quarterback twice.

Senior Randy Fillingame led the defense with a whopping 13 tackles. Two-thirds of the team's tackles were unassisted, once again showing strong fundamentals for the Bearcats defense.

Running back Rashad Broadnax also delivered a dominant performance. Carrying the ball 26 times, he rushed for 140 yards, including a 7-yard touchdown to punctuate an eight play, 80-yard drive in the third quarter. After the score, he ran for a two-point conversion and personally outscored Cairo 8 to 7. The remaining touchdown came in the fourth quarter on a Tevin McCray 5-yard rushing touchdown, followed by a Caleb Harris extra point. The final score was 15-7, an important early victory for Bainbridge.[30]

The game did give rise to some concerns, especially the four fumbles by the Bainbridge offense. The three sacks allowed and the 4-of-13 third-down conversion rate were also worthy of attention. Twelve penalties for 121 yards seems bad, but with Cairo penalized even more (14 for 134),[31] it might have said more about whistle-happy officials than the quality of the play.

Numbers aside, the Bearcats had just defeated one of the state's best AAAA teams, and had shut out its opponents for seven out of the eight quarters. The season now held some seriously good potential.

Sadly, during the next week, the players received news that meant the season also held the potential for tragedy. The Ryan kids were an important part of the team. Michael was a starting wide receiver, and Andrew was a freshman kicker. Their dad, Jeremy, had coached many of the Bainbridge Bearcats on youth league teams in years past. "If I hadn't coached them, I had probably coached against them and knew just about all of their families," he explained.[32]

30   Game statistics provided by the Bainbridge High School Bearcats coaching staff, and specifically by statistician Chip Ariail.
31   Id.
32   Jeremy Ryan (dad of Bainbridge of two players) in discussion with the

So on August 28, when Jeremy Ryan was diagnosed with cancer, the news placed the family and childhood paradigm of Michael and Andrew Ryan in jeopardy. Would he survive? What types of treatments would he undergo? What effects would the treatments have on him? What would their family do?

The Ryan boys battled grief and the need to continue with daily life as their dad began the battle for his very life. Thankfully, they did not have to fight their battle alone. "Their coaches and teammates were really there for them," Jeremy Ryan recalled. "They loved my sons and stood with them."[33]

Along with the coaches and players, another member of the team reached out to the Ryan family. He had joined the team because of a lunch in 2017. Coach Jeff Littleton mentioned to Bobby Barber, the Touchdown Club president at the time, that he would like to bring in a minister to serve as a team chaplain. Littleton explained that he wanted to accent the spiritual development of the players, along with their football experience and personal discipline. Faith was an important part of his and his family's lives, and also to many of the coaches.[34]

Barber suggested Steve Brooks, the associate pastor at Climax Baptist Church in the area and a longtime volunteer with the Fellowship of Christian Athletes. As a former high school football player, Brooks would likely become a natural fit with the team and a source of guidance and inspiration, Barber believed.

Barber set up a lunch involving himself, Brooks, Littleton and Coach Ryan Kineard. They discussed the spiritual outreach to the players, and the philosophy of the chaplain's role with the team. Ultimately, Littleton offered Brooks a ten-minute devotional time with the players before each game. Brooks was impressed with the coaches' dedication to every aspect of the players' lives. "These guys really care about the individual players," he recalled.

So Brooks reached out to the Ryan family and made himself available, as always, for them or anyone else who needed

author, December 3, 2019.
33   Id.
34   Rev. Steve Brooks (Bainbridge team chaplain) in discussion with the author, December 3, 2019.

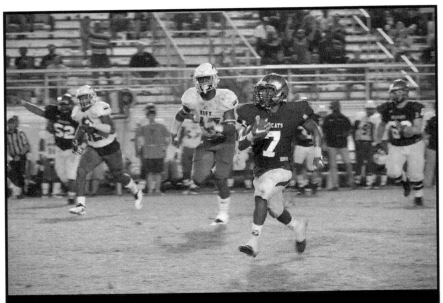

Aaron Spivie, the team's leading receiver during the 2018 season, sprints out into the open field against the Tift County defense.

to talk. Every member of the team was devoted to their team-mates and the dad they respected so much.

The Ryan diagnosis might have been the first time the 2018 team dealt with trauma, but it would not be the last.

Bainbridge vs. Lincoln of Tallahassee
August 30, 2018

Nobody can accuse Coach Jeff Littleton or his Bain-bridge team of playing a cupcake schedule. For the third game of the season, the Bearcats took on Lincoln High School of Tallahassee, Florida.

Bleacher Report has named Lincoln one of the top-five football factories in America for producing future top-notch college and professional players. Sports fans watching football coverage on ESPN have seen Lincoln alumnus Kevin Carter, the University of Florida All-American and longtime NFL star, who serves as an expert on college football.[35]

Lincoln's reputation as a factory for football stars has

35   *Pro Football Reference*, "Kevin Carter," https://www.pro-football-reference. com/players/C/CartKe00.htm. Retrieved February 20, 2019.

been well-earned. Boo Williams, P.J. Daniels, and the four-time Pro-Bowl legend Antonio Cromartie are just some of the legends produced by the school.

So would the Bainbridge boys continue their perfect record by defeating the football factory from Florida?

The Bearcats issued another defeat, but unfortunately, this time the victim was their own team. The victory on the scoreboard looked like a blowout, but for Bainbridge, the loss was in no small part self-induced.

The Bainbridge defense held Lincoln on its first three drives, but still trailed 7-0 on the scoreboard because a Bearcats' fumble at their own 13-yard-line became a scoop-and-score touchdown. Bryce Worthy and Randy Fillingame paced the defense with eight tackles apiece.[36] Three-fourths of all the tackles were solo, once again a good measure of the defense efficiency.

Giving up no sustained scoring drives in the first half, the defense allowed one long touchdown run and went into the halftime break trailing 14-0.

Bainbridge powered its way to an effective rushing attack, with two different running backs running for over 90 yards. Rashad Broadnax once again led the way with 97 yards on 19 carries, an outstanding 5.1 yards-per-carry. Tevin McCray had 93 yards on 13 carries, for a whopping 7.2 yards per carry.

The Bainbridge ground attack was not stopped by Lincoln. Unfortunately, they didn't have to, as the Bearcats did that to themselves. Five fumbles (two were lost), became drive stoppers for Bainbridge. Add the two interceptions thrown and four sacks surrendered, and the game became an early Christmas present for Lincoln.

Bainbridge vs. Brooks County
September 7, 2018

As the season rolled into September, the month's first Friday brought another game and another playoff team, Brooks

---

36   Bainbridge Football Home, *MaxPreps.com*, https://www.maxpreps.com/games/8-30-2018/football-fall-18/bainbridge-vs-lincoln.htm?c=NHC78c4fl06Y-5ijWMrSA2Q#tab=box-score&schoolid=. Retrieved October 9, 2019.

County High School. Bainbridge traveled to face the Trojans in Quitman, Georgia, the home of great wins, great players and great history.

Just about everyone in America has at least one small connection to Quitman. At 19 High Street in Quitman, at the Simpson Tavern, a local educator and organist named James Pierpont authored the wintertime classic song, "Jingle Bells." Anyone who has ever heard or sung the song can thank Quitman, Georgia, for producing the talented Mr. Pierpont, who was also the uncle of the great American Wall Street tycoon, John Pierpont Morgan.[37]

And then there's the football tradition. The 1994 Brooks County Trojans not only captured the state title but also had its star player, then-junior Marcus Stroud, featured on the cover of *Sports Illustrated* magazine. Stroud went on to a great career as a star player for the University of Georgia Bulldogs, a first-round choice in the NFL draft, and a ten-year star in the league.[38]

In the world of football, there's an old saying that "defense travels." That means that it's more likely for a strong defense to perform well in hostile arenas than it is for an offense. Reasons for that include dealing with crowd noise, keeping an eye on the play clock that might be in a different location, and orchestrating an offense in unfamiliar surroundings.

For the Bainbridge defense, giving up just over 11 points-per-game heading into the Brooks County game, the challenge was to contain a Trojans offense that had scored a whopping 80 points in its first two games. Brooks County would average right at 30 points-per-game for the entire season and score almost twice as many points as they surrendered.

And that's exactly what they did. For three of the four quarters, the Bearcats defense shutout Brooks County. Unfortunately, the two touchdowns, along with a self-induced safety on special teams, was just enough for the playoff-bound Tro-

37   Klein, Christopher, "8 things you might not know about Jingle Bells," *History.com*, December 16, 2016. https://www.history.com/news/8-things-you-may-not-know-about-jingle-bells. Retrieved January 19, 2019.
38   *Pro Football Reference*, "Marcus Stroud," https://www.pro-football-reference.com/players/S/StroMa01.htm. Retrieved February 20, 2019.

jans to squeak out a home-field win, 15-13.[39]

Other than the safety, the contest was a completely even game. Each team scored 13 offensive points. Each team gained 132 first downs. Each team lost two fumbles. Each team had exactly 52 yards in negative-yardage plays. Each team punted six times, and they had almost identical total yardages (230 for Bainbridge and 234 for Brooks County).

Randy Fillingame followed on the previous two weeks' performances with another great game. Against Brooks County, Fillingame had eight tackles, with an impressive seven of them unassisted. Most importantly, he had no less than five tackles-for loss. Roman Harrison also delivered a dominating performance with four tackles-for-loss, and six of his seven tackles being unassisted.[40]

Rashad Broadnax once again led the ground attack for the Bearcats with 84 yards (and a net of 67). Caleb McDowell and Deyon Bouie each averaged eight yards-per-carry. Bouie added an interception to his stats for the game.

Jaylen Peterson led the aerial attack with four catches for 33 yards and an 11-yard touchdown thrown by quarterback Quayde Hawkins.[41]

The game brought a disappointing result, but may have also given rise to the optimism of knowing that only a few plays separated them from another win over a playoff team.

Bainbridge vs. Crisp County
September 21, 2018

The season of facing playoff games continued, as Bainbridge squared off with the Crisp County Cougars from Cordele. Like so many other South Georgia towns, Cordele has carved its unique history with athletes and achievers. Children of Cordele have gone on to become NFL players, NBA players,

39   Game statistics provided by the Bainbridge High School Bearcats coaching staff, and specifically by statistician Chip Ariail.
40   Bainbridge Football Home, *MaxPreps.com*, https://www.maxpreps.com/games/9-7-2018/football-fall-18/bainbridge-vs-brooks-county.htm?c=zX8lo-D6a9kWZPasO76n16g#tab=box-score&schoolid=. Retrieved July 18, 2019.
41   Game statistics provided by the Bainbridge High School Bearcats coaching staff, and specifically by statistician Chip Ariail.

Olympic athletes, a White House Press Secretary, a best-selling author, and famous musicians.

On paper, the game matched equal performances from playoff-bound teams. On paper, the game was a defensive struggle. Both teams finished the game with only 10 first downs. Only 12 yards separated the total yardage of the two teams. Combined, the two teams went a dreadful 4-for-22 on third-down conversions.

As the fourth quarter began, the Bainbridge defense had only surrendered one score, and the Bearcats trailed 9-0 (the Cougars had registered a safety in the first quarter).

And then, with 9:46 remaining in the game, the most important stat of the game became the number four.

That's four, as in four Bainbridge turnovers on their last four possessions of the game. It began with the pick-six by Crisp County's Tubby Spivey, a 42-yarder that broke the game open at the 9:46 mark.[42]

The game ended in a painful, 23-0 loss that did not reflect how the entire game was played. Senior Roman Harrison made an impressive 13 tackles, tying him with Randy Fillingame's effort against Brooks County for the most individual tackles in a game so far in the season. Harrison added four tackles-for-loss. Junior Amari Peterson added eight tackles and a tackle-for-loss.[43]

Rashad Broadnax rushed for 47 yards on just seven carries, pacing the ground game. Adrian Cooper led the aerial attack with four receptions, while Aaron Spivie and Caleb McDowell each had three catches. All three averaged over eight yards-per-reception for the game.

Despite some nice statistics, the game brought a painful loss, and an embarrassing loss. The atmosphere in the locker room reflected both the result of the game and the overall record so far.

"That was probably as close to a defeated locker room as they had," team chaplain Steve Brooks recalled. "The rest of the season would be determined by the ability of the coaches

42 Id.
43 Bainbridge Football Home, *MaxPreps.com*, https://www.maxpreps.com/games/9-21-2018/football-fall-18/bainbridge-vs-crisp-county.htm?c=lBfhjHS-GqUSFREhB174tNQ#tab=box-score&schoolid=. Retrieved October 13, 2019.

to inspire hard work and improvement despite how the season began."[44]

Bainbridge vs. Tift County
September 28, 2018

After a grueling schedule of playoff teams each week, the excessively young Bainbridge team needed a gimme, a game against a sub-par team that would allow the younger players to gain valuable experience, hopefully with a large lead against a smaller school.

Instead, Bainbridge faced another playoff team as it did just about every week. Tift County was not only headed to the playoffs, the Blue Devils had already defeated mighty Valdosta by two touchdowns, and had smacked down Worth County 46-6.[45] Tifton, like so many other southern Georgia towns, also brought a rich legacy of success in individual and team sports. Placing athletes in the NFL, Major League Baseball, the LPGA and top college programs, the Blue Devil players had been raised in a culture of achievement.

This was not the opponent for a young team to face after a tough, self-induced loss. Bainbridge jumped out to a quick lead as Caleb McDowell sprinted for a 70-yard touchdown.

Two Blue Devil scores, a touchdown and field goal, gave them the lead in the second quarter. Late in the first half, Bainbridge began a drive at the Tift County 34-yard-line, and it became a one-play drive when Aaron Spivie broke a 34-yard touchdown run.

As the first half ended, Bainbridge took a 14-10 lead into the intermission. Things seemed to be going well, and the Bearcats took the opening drive of the second half and went 53 yards in 10 plays. Unfortunately, the drive ended with an unsuccessful fourth-down conversion play, the second of three in the game for Bainbridge. Tift County countered with a long

44   Rev. Steve Brooks (Bainbridge team chaplain) in discussion with the author, December 3, 2019.
45   Tift County 2018 Football Schedule, *MaxPreps.com*, https://www.max-preps.com/high-schools/tift-county-blue-devils-(tifton,ga)/football-fall-18/schedule.htm. Retrieved October 9, 2019.

The only thing greater than the number of Bainbridge fans who support their team is their vocal support at games. Fans truly can make a difference in games, but only if the cheerleaders inspire and direct that energy in the right ways and at the right times.

drive of their own, an 11-play, 76-yard drive[46] to take the lead with the only score of the third quarter.

It was the first of three consecutive scoring drives for the Blue Devils and that was how the game ended, with a 31-14 disappointment.

Once again, the game's stats did not reflect the scoring margin. The teams had almost identical total yardage (236 to 230), and the same number of penalties. Bainbridge had no turnovers, while Tift County lost two fumbles.

Caleb McDowell shredded the Blue Devil defense for 112 yards, and Aaron Spivie added a 34-yard touchdown on his only ground carry, to go along with his 29 yards in kick re-

---

46   Game statistics provided by the Bainbridge High School Bearcats coaching staff, and specifically by statistician Chip Ariail.

turns and an 8-yard reception.[47]

Bryce Worthy continued his excellent senior season with 13 tackles (three for loss). Roman Harrison added eight tackles, four of them for lost yardage. Anthony Brooks and Randy Fillingame each added seven stops.

The key number may well have been the 0-for-3 on fourth-down conversions, but that probably didn't help any of the Bearcats handle the loss any better.

One of the most telling results of the game came afterward, when Coach Littleton spoke with Mark and Connie Mitchell. As leaders of the Bainbridge Touchdown Club and parents of two players, the Mitchells were as tuned-in to the team and its success as anyone. "We can still win the region," Littleton remarked confidently.[48]

Bainbridge vs. Veterans
October 5, 2018

Another week brought another playoff-destined opponent for the Bainbridge Bearcats. Less than ten years old, Veterans High School has already become an outstanding school in Houston County and Warner Robins. Situated near Robins Air Force Base, the school includes a large percentage of children of military families.

While the nation's defense is the work of the area, the Bainbridge defense controlled much of the game. Led by its seniors, the Bearcats "D" racked up a whopping 12 tackles-for-loss. Bryce Worthy had ten tackles, and Randy Fillingame added eight tackles and a 54-yard pick-six interception return for a touchdown. The defense added two sacks in holding the Veterans to only one score in each half.[49]

Bainbridge head coach Jeff Littleton and his staff flexed the game plan, placing more responsibility in the hands of his team's aerial attack. Quarterback Quayde Hawkins passed for 183 yards, and a 48-yard pass by Caleb McDowell gave the

47   Id.
48   Jeff Littleton (Bainbridge head football coach) in discussion with the author, December 3, 2019.
49   Game statistics provided by the Bainbridge High School Bearcats coaching staff, and specifically by statistician Chip Ariail.

Bearcats 231 passing yards.[50]

The Bainbridge offense also racked up 18 first downs, easily the most in any game to that point of the season.

With the way the Bearcats defense played, the 17-point outburst in the second quarter was more than enough to win the game for Bainbridge. With 10 tackles (eight unassisted), Bryce Worthy led the defensive effort. He was joined by Randy Fillingame (eight tackles, four for loss), Anthony Brooks (seven tackles) and Roman Harrison (six tackles).[51]

---

50   Id.
51   Veterans 2018 Football Schedule, *MaxPreps.com*, https://www.maxpreps. com/games/10-5-2018/football-fall-18/bainbridge-vs-veterans.htm?c=ZL59Ex-KqwUaQhE_cQrRHPQ#tab=recap&schoolid=. Retrieved February 20, 2019.

Chapter 2

A Perfect Storm

"Bainbridge Georgia looks like a war zone. It may be several days before you see someone to help just please bear with us...."

--George McMillan

Hurricane Michael was a massive storm as it raged into the Gulf of Mexico. Before landfall at the Florida panhandle, it was almost as large as the entire state of Florida.

"I remember exactly what I was doing."

Those words ring true for most Americans who were alive during the September 11, 2001 attacks, the first moon landing, the Kennedy assassination, or the attack on Pearl Harbor. Typically, those events bring enormous importance and an equal measure of surprise.

For the people of Bainbridge, and the young members of its high school football team, a catastrophic event lay only a few days ahead in their future. Just about everyone would long remember where they were when the disaster arrived.

For most students at Bainbridge, the Monday brought the beginning of a typical high school week. Tests were studied for, taken, and prayed over. There was plenty of creative writing, too. Some of those words were composed for class assignments, and much of it on smartphones.

The members of the Bainbridge Bearcats football team were already focusing, after some disappointing losses, on

30

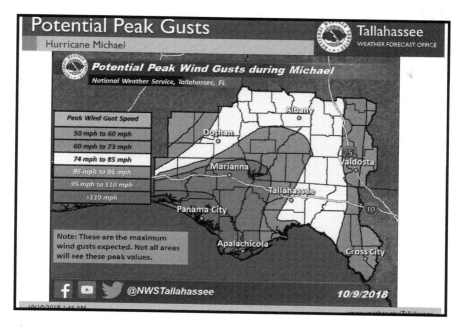

Potential Peak Gusts
Hurricane Michael
Tallahassee
WEATHER FORECAST OFFICE

Potential Peak Wind Gusts during Michael
National Weather Service, Tallahassee, FL

Peak Wind Gust Speed
50 mph to 60 mph
60 mph to 73 mph
74 mph to 85 mph
85 mph to 95 mph
95 mph to 110 mph
>110 mph

Note: These are the maximum wind gusts expected. Not all areas will see these peak values.

@NWSTallahassee
10/9/2018

their upcoming game against Veterans High School.

If anything about the day seemed stormy, it was the news headlines across America. America, already a deeply divided nation, was suffering through a combative and hostile confirmation fight for a U.S. Supreme Court justice. The raging accusations flew. The investigations intensified. The politicians postured.

On that day, at least one problem was being solved. The United States and Canada were working hard to resolve their trade conflict over the NAFTA treaty, and a tentative breakthrough agreement had been reached.[52]

For most high school kids, like most adults, news headlines of strife were remote events, as most people remain most concerned about what's happening in their own community.

For the Bainbridge Bearcats and their passionate fan base, the football season had already become a storm of disappointment and regret.

Monday, October 1st brought a new day, a new school week, and a new month. Maybe the newness would help fortify the support of the team by its fan base.

52   Headlines, October 1, 2018, *DemocracyNow.org*, https://www.democracynow.org/2018/10/1/headlines, Retrieved July 18, 2019.

The season of football, more than the calendar, was the thing that really needed a new beginning. The weekend had brought another loss; their losing streak now totaled four in a row. In their most recent two games, they had been outscored 54-to-14. For the Bearcats players, those headlines might have seemed more immediate and stormy than anything involving a trade agreement or a judge.

Despite everything happening on that first day of the new month, October's biggest story, on that very morning, was beginning to brew, well over a thousand miles away.

On that same day, a storm arose from a low-pressure front in the southwestern area of the Caribbean. From day one, it was a different type of storm. Over 85 percent of all hurricanes that hit the United States originate off the coast of Africa, so its ultimate path wouldn't be the first unusual thing about it. Nor would its ferocity, which would become historic by the time it hit the United States.

As storms often do, especially in the warm Caribbean waters, it grew in size and intensity. This storm, ultimately named Michael, developed more slowly than many, not reaching tropical depression for almost a week, on October 7.

On the 7th, however, the storm morphed from a slowly developing mass into a fast and dangerous storm. By the next day, October 8, it had already grown into a tropical storm. In just one more day, Michael had quickly developed into a hurricane by the time it reached western Cuba.[53]

Then came the most dangerous moment.

Most of the time, the most dangerous and deadly hurricanes travel through the Gulf of Mexico. Its warm waters provide fuel for the storm, strengthening both its speed and its ferocity. One of the most famous recent examples was Hurricane Katrina, which devastated New Orleans and much of southern Mississippi, along with parts of Alabama.

On October 8, the NOAA NWS National Hurricane Center issued an announcement that began with the following warning: _____

53   John L. Beven II, Robbie Berg, and Andrew Hagan (April 19, 2019). "Tropical Cyclone Report: Hurricane Michael" (PDF). National Hurricane Center. NOAA. Retrieved May 1, 2019. https://www.nhc.noaa.gov/data/tcr/AL142018_Michael.pdf

The street sign at the intersection of Broughton and Clarke vividly portrays the upheaval of lives, families, and the entire community of Bainbridge,.

...CENTER OF MICHAEL PASSING NEAR THE WESTERN TIP OF CUBA...

...HEAVY RAINFALL AND STRONG WINDS SPREADING ACROSS WESTERN CUBA...

...RISK OF LIFE-THREATENING STORM SURGE...HEAVY RAIN-FALL...AND

DANGEROUS WINDS INCREASING FOR THE NORTHEAST-ERN GULF COAST...[54]

So, after hammering Cuba, Michael traveled into the Gulf of Mexico and darted toward America's Deep South.

It was now a race against time. Families prepared for the damage that was surely on the way. The approaching

54 Facebook.com, Decatur County EMA Bainbridge, Georgia, https://www.facebook.com/Decatur-County-EMA-Bainbridge-GA-1421794984594631/?__tn__=%2Cd%2CP-R&eid=ARCxj--jxlnEjeTrmhwoVWLV-sgdXT1nujJUTFSm-MRvSq__MFPZ8wx9W7SE3KR8aD7Xsa_oipYjEgy6l

Local officials from all levels of government meet to plan the aggressive response to the devastation caused by Hurricane Michael. The teamwork between the county government, city government, and private individuals was one of the primary reasons the community recovered as well as it did.

storm provoked states of emergency by governments, including Georgia, where Governor Nathan Deal declared a state of emergency for 92 counties.[55] The expected sales and resulting shortages followed, creating high demand and low supplies of bottled water, canned food, and the typical things that people buy before storms.

On the same day, the Decatur County Emergency Management Authority issued the following directive:

Emergency Preparations and Supplies:

• Make sure you have enough food and water for at least 3-4 days. Fill your bathtub with water.

• Secure outdoor furniture, flags, and trash cans. Remove dead limbs and yard debris that could damage property.

• Take care of your outdoor pets. Bring them inside or into a secure building. Make sure they have enough food for several days.

• If you need medicine, get your prescriptions filled beforehand. Have extra oxygen or other necessary medical supplies/

---

55   Id.

devices on hand.

• Supplies to have on hand: flashlights and batteries, first aid kit, battery powered radio, manual can opener, canned food, fire extinguisher, generator.[56]

Time was of the essence. Every person, family, and organization was moving as quickly as they could to prepare. The regional Red Cross met with city officials to plan the opening of the coliseum as a post-storm shelter. Local churches also made plans for "good Samaritan" shelters to open as well.

The growing power, propelled by the Gulf's warm waters, was the reason that the tropical storm became a hurricane, and then a major hurricane, within 24 hours. Experts predicted that fast-traveling storm could hit the Florida panhandle the next day, on October 10. It carried the potential to grow into a Category 5 hurricane, but those were rare indeed. No Category 5 hurricane had hit the United States in over 25 years, and no storm at that level had ever hit the Florida panhandle.

The people of Bainbridge fully understood how to prepare for hurricanes. One of the many great things about living there was having the best of both worlds: it carries all of the benefits of a small-town, Southern lifestyle, but lies only a quick drive away from the sparkling white beaches of Florida.

Living that close to the beach means paying attention to tropical storms and hurricanes, and preparing accordingly. So while getting ready for a possible hurricane was never routine, it was still nothing outside the normal October near the Gulf Coast.

But there was nothing normal about Hurricane Michael. By the time the news broke that over 200,000 Cubans were without power, the public was on notice that this storm was a whopper.

That afternoon, the official hurricane warning was issued for Bainbridge:

HURRICANE WARNING HAS BEEN ISSUED FOR DECATUR COUNTY FOR THE NEXT 36 HOURS.
...HURRICANE WARNING IN EFFECT...

---

56   Id.

35

A Hurricane Warning means hurricane-force winds are expected somewhere within this area within the next 36 hours.

* LOCATIONS AFFECTED
- Bainbridge
* WIND
- LATEST LOCAL FORECAST: Equivalent Tropical Storm force wind
- Peak Wind Forecast: 45-55 mph with gusts to 75 mph
- Window for Tropical Storm force winds: Wednesday morning until early Thursday morning
- POTENTIAL THREAT TO LIFE AND PROPERTY: Potential for wind 74 to 110 mph[57]

This time, the experts were right. For the first time in recorded history, a Category 5 hurricane made a direct hit on the panhandle of Florida. In fact, it became the first Category 5 hurricane to hit the continental United States since Hurricane Andrew in 1992.

During the lunch hour of October 10, Michael reached the coast, smashing directly into the small town of Mexico Beach, Florida, with winds clocked at 160 miles per hour. The results were almost unimaginable. Brock Long, an administrator for the Federal Emergency Management Agency (FEMA), described Mexico Beach as "wiped out." Government officials began calling the town Ground Zero. In Mexico Beach, 1,584 buildings out of 1,692 in the town were reported damaged, with 809 of those reported destroyed.[58] Most homes and buildings in Mexico Beach were wiped out indeed. The town's pier was simply washed away into the violent ocean.

For the people of Bainbridge, the storm's ferocity was the first of two items of bad news. The other was its path, which hit Mexico Beach traveling a northeastern path that would ultimately include Bainbridge.

The fourth strongest storm in American history was

---

57   Id.
58   John L. Beven II, Robbie Berg, and Andrew Hagan (April 19, 2019). "Tropical Cyclone Report: Hurricane Michael" (PDF). National Hurricane Center. NOAA. Retrieved May 1, 2019. https://www.nhc.noaa.gov/data/tcr/AL142018_Michael.pdf.

Hurricane Michael

By the Numbers

5

...As in a Category 5. Michael became the first Category 5 hurricane to hit the continental United States since Hurricane Andrew in 1992.

14

Many in Bainbridge lived without a power source for 14 days after the hurricane struck, according to interviews.

35

Hurricane Michael claimed 35 lives in the United States, including an 11-year-old child in nearby Seminole County.

98

Parts of U.S. Highway 98 were simply missing as a result of Hurricane Michael's fury.

3 billion

Georgia's agricultural crops sustained $3 billion in damages as a result of Hurricane Michael.

A Bainbridge home lies literally sliced into two pieces as the result of a massive tree crashing through its roof. The sight of a large tree so easily uprooted shows the fury of the historically powerful Hurricane Michael.

Workers prepare to clear away destroyed trees in front of a home that stands only partially visible behind the debris left in the wake of Hurricane Michael. Local governments and volunteers spent many months cleaning up the massive quantities of debris that covered much of the city.

headed directly at them.

The results in the Florida panhandle and the southern part of Georgia were devastating. Entire sections of U.S. Highway 98, one of America's most scenic routes, were missing. One broadcasting company in nearby Panama City which owned multiple radio stations, sustained such overwhelming damage to its towers and facilities that the company simply closed down its operations after the storm had passed.

In Georgia alone, the storm damage reached staggering totals. The agricultural losses totaled close to $3 billion. In Decatur County, home to Bainbridge, 85 percent of the pecan crop was lost, according to a report in the *Atlanta Journal Constitution*. The poultry industry was also hit hard, losing over 2 million chickens in the storm. According to reports a year after the storm by Georgia Public Radio, the state's cotton crop sustained over $300 million in damages.

Tragically, Michael claimed 35 lives in the United States, including an 11-year-old child in nearby Seminole County. A few days after the storm had hit and passed, the funeral for Sarah Radney, who was killed at her grandparents' home in the Lake Seminole area, was held in Cairo.[59]

After blowing through Georgia, North Carolina, and Virginia, Michael was not finished. The storm shot out into the Atlantic Ocean, regained its strength, and headed for halfway across the globe to Europe. On October 14, Michael again made landfall, this time on the coast of Portugal before finally dissipating in the skies over Spain.

A return to normalcy

The hurricane had finally passed, but that was merely the first part of the storm in many ways. The tasks facing the Bainbridge community, and the entire region of the state, were almost beyond belief.

There was no time, however, to consider the enormity of the tasks because there were too many urgent needs. The entire community sprang into action. The Georgia Baptist Mis-

59   Hassanein, Nada, "'God took her home': Killed by Hurricane Michael, Georgia 11-year-old had a beautiful heart," *Tallahassee Democrat,* October 20, 2018. https://www.tallahassee.com/story/news/2018/10/20/georgia-family-mourns-death-11-year-old-girl-hurricane-michael/1687610002/. Retrieved April 18, 2019.

sion began helping to remove trees from structures and to put tarp on the exposed areas of homes. The Bainbridge Church of God became a safe haven shelter. So too did St. Paul's Church, on Fowlston Road. The Jones-Wheat Elementary School Gymnasium was opened as a post-storm shelter. Needed water and meals-ready-to-eat were quickly made available at the Bainbridge Southwest Regional Technical College.[60]

Local officials warned the public to stay off the roads, as many roads were impassible and first responders were needed for storm-related emergencies rather than helping stranded motorists who ventured out too early after the storm.

The city imposed a curfew between 1 and 7 a.m., mostly because of power outages and travel problems but also because of some robberies. Two days after the storm had passed, the power company estimated that Bainbridge would have power restored within four days. Two senior players for the Bearcats recalled that their homes lost power for at least two weeks.

Local officials announced certain sites for people to drop off household garbage, and other sites for people to dump debris. Southwest Baptist Church and the Salvation Army became important locations providing meals. Bags of ice were made available in the vacant lot beside the Home Depot, with a two-bag limit per vehicle.

According to an article by *BuzzFeed*, "The only functioning gas station in town operated on an industrial-sized generator that was there for emergency personnel and first responders."

George McMillan, a local public safety official, may have put it best: "Bainbridge Georgia looks like a war zone. It may be several days before you see someone to help just please bear with us...."[61]

In many ways, McMillan was right. Similarly to a wartime attack, the enemy named Hurricane Michael came, in the

60   Facebook.com, Decatur County EMA Bainbridge, Georgia, https://www. facebook.com/Decatur-County-EMA-Bainbridge-GA-1421794984594631/?__ tn__=%2Cd%2CP-R&eid=ARCxj--jxlnEjeTrmhwoVWLV-sgdXT1nujJUTFSm-MRvSq__MFPZ8wx9W7SE3KR8aD7Xsa_oipYjEgy6l
61   Ansari, Talal, ""Like A War Zone": A Georgia City 100 Miles Inland Was Pulverized By Hurricane Michael," *BuzzFeed.com*, October 11, 2018. https://

Biblical description, to steal, kill, and destroy. In its wake, the people of Bainbridge found many shattered homes and lives.

McMillan wasn't the only one who described the town as resembling a war zone after the storm. Bainbridge players Michael and Andrew Ryan were at a Tallahassee hospital with their parents because of treatment complications with their dad, Jeremy, a cancer patient. With the storm approaching and heading right toward Bainbridge, they got the doctor's permission to head northward and quickly prepare their house as well as possible. Afterward, they headed to LaGrange so they could be near medical attention if that became necessary. On October 10, the Ryans began receiving texted photos showing the damage, but that could not prepare them for the vivid reality of their hometown when they returned.

Coach Brian Hill, his wife Liz, and their daughters stayed with Liz's parents during the hurricane. When Brian first returned, he gave virtually the same description as the Ryan family and George McMillan: "It was a war zone."[62]

The descriptions ring eerily similar to those of New Orleans natives after Hurricane Katrina. James Adams, a local businessman who had evacuated his family from New Orleans, returned to find an unrecognizable neighborhood that he called home. He also described it as a war zone. "It was like I had driven to Beirut."[63]

Coach Joe Dollar didn't have the opportunity to see his lifelong hometown on the day after the hurricane struck. He couldn't even make it to the end of his driveway, even on foot. The yard was a big mass of crushed trees and limbs. Those trees weren't the only thing in the yard that was crushed, as one tree fell directly on what had once been his wife's car.[64]

Post Searchlight managing editor Powell Cobb didn't have to drive into town to first witness the devastation. "I lived in a building downtown that was falling apart around me during Hurricane Michael. I was finally able to escape it around midnight with

www.buzzfeednews.com/article/talalansari/like-a-war-zone-a-georgia-city-100-miles-inland-was. Retrieved on September 27, 2019.
62   Brian Hill (Bainbridge defensive football coach) in discussion with the author, November 23, 2019.
63   Ward, Tom, "The Dirty Thirty: America's Greatest High School Football Rivalries," First Street Books (2012).
64   Dollar, Joe (Bainbridge defensive football coach) in discussion with the author, December 16, 2019.

the help of Bainbridge Public Safety, and I drove my smashed-up car to The *Post-Searchlight* office with a sleeping bag and pillow to try and get a little rest," he recalled.[65]

When the morning mercifully arrived, Powell left the newspaper office and walked out into the biggest story in the town's history. "Some places didn't look familiar anymore," he explained. "Massive oak trees that had stood the test of centuries were uprooted, turning large stretches of sidewalk and streets into a crumbled mess of cement. Folks everywhere were in their yards with chainsaws, trying to cut their way out from the jumble of trees blocking their driveways and the roads around the city. Homes and businesses had their roofs caved in and windows smashed. It was like nothing I had ever seen with my own eyes."[66]

Anyone who underestimates the value and power of local newspapers should have been in Bainbridge in the aftermath of the storm. For many, if not most in the area, their phones were the source of news and the *Post Searchlight* was the source for communicating anything of importance. According to multiple sources, the newspaper's impressive social media following allowed the people of Bainbridge and Decatur County to learn of shelters, food, and passable roads.

Chainsaws roared into fallen trees. Families walked around trees in their bedrooms as they began covering holes in their homes. Adults and kids alike longed for restored cell phone coverage so they could check on loved ones.

By the time of the first post-storm team meeting, the Bearcats Touchdown Club had already sprung into action. Mark and Connie Mitchell, the present and past presidents of the group, began planning dinner for the team each night, just to make sure that all of the kids were provided healthy meals during this unique season in their lives.

So the storm had hardly passed, and the football players were already being cared for. The scene was set for togetherness.

---

65 Powell Cobb (*Post Searchlight* managing editor) in discussion with the author, December 8, 2019.
66 Id.

Chapter 3

Heart and Soul

"People in small towns, much more than in cities, share a destiny."

--Richard Russo

Ground Zero

It was the day that Bainbridge became Ground Zero.

When the Hurricane Michael crashed into South Georgia, it scored a direct hit on Decatur County and the city of Bainbridge. Media from across the state and nation descended on the area for reconnaissance and reporting. *Buzzfeed* profiled the damage, accurately calling Bainbridge a "war zone" in a national headline. Georgia Public Radio covered the damage extensively and followed up in the intervening months.

Georgia Governor Nathan Deal called Bainbridge Ground Zero for the hurricane's path through the Peach State. Most Americans now associate the term Ground Zero with the site of the September 11 terrorist attacks in the Lower Manhattan area of New York, so the term brought a meaningful description of how the hurricane had affected the area.

But the hurricane didn't just smash directly into a city; it hit a community and a culture.

Understanding how and why the community and its youth responded as they did is not complicated, but it's best done through the lens of the city's history. The iconic Southern movie *Forrest Gump* features an expression by Gump's mother, played by Sally Field, to explain life to her intellectually challenged son: "Stupid is, as stupid does."

The same can be said for communities as well as people. Likewise, the same can also be said for courage, for determination, and for their refusal to quit.

For the city of Bainbridge, it started with day one.

Remember who you are
"Remember who you are."

44

Across America, children and teenagers hear those words before departing for school, ball games, hanging out with friends, or out-of-town trips.

The meaning is simple. If you remain mindful of your identity as a person, the family who raised you, your school, hometown, or the things you claim to believe, your actions will naturally flow from that.

In 2013, Stan Killough, then the athletic director at Bainbridge High School introduced Jeff Littleton as the new head coach of the Bearcats. As a native of Bainbridge, Killough fully understood what the Bainbridge name meant. "One thing that made Coach Littleton stand out as a candidate was his determination to build championship people as zealously as he would seek to win championships," Killough explained. "Coach always said he wanted to coach these kids in life so they would become part of the world's solutions rather than part of the problem." Killough knows plenty about a championship culture, growing up in Bainbridge and then playing college baseball at the University of Alabama.[67]

67   Stan Killough (former athletic director at Bainbridge High School) in discussion with the author, December 14, 2019.

The Georgia National Guard established stations to efficiently distribute needed supplies to areas affected by Hurricane Michael. Pictured, above, are stations in the Bainbridge area where citizens could receive packages of bottled water. Georgia Governor Nathan Deal had referred to Bainbridge as Ground Zero of damage.

After Killough introduced him as the new head coach, Littleton explained that he had sought the job because he had always known what it meant to play against Bainbridge. "I looked forward to playing Bainbridge because they hit hard, and we knew what we would get."[68]

For Littleton, the Bainbridge name has meant a lot for 30 years. For the United States of America, that name has meant fierce bravery for the past 200 years. William Bainbridge was born into a world of war and strife, in 1774, as his father was a doctor and a British Loyalist who sided with England during the American Revolution.[69]

Growing up in a nation at war, especially with a father supporting the other side, probably made William Bainbridge mature at a younger age than typical boys of the day. Before his teenage years had ended, Bainbridge had become an ac-

---

68   New BHS Head Football Coach Littleton Addresses the Team, YouTube video, 15:32, March 22, 2013. https://www.youtube.com/watch?v=TeDJ7G-5mX_U&feature=youtu.be. Retrieved April 18, 2019.
69   National Park Service, "William Bainbridge," https://www.nps.gov/people/william-bainbridge.htm. Retrieved November 26, 2018.

Above (left) the path of Young Stribling's life took him from his Bainbridge childhood, to a traveling Vaudeville act with his family, to a record-setting boxing career. Above (right) Miriam Hopkins developed her performing skills as a child in the St. John's Episcopal Church in Bainbridge, and later became a Hollywood star.

complished and highly respected boat captain. Also, while still a teenager, he had successfully battled and put down a mutiny on another ship.

When the U.S. Navy was founded in 1798, Bainbridge was appointed one of the first naval officers and commissioned to the schooner boat, *Retaliation*. As his reputation grew, Bainbridge led ships into multiple wars on behalf of the young United States of America, becoming one of the nation's leading men of the seas.

Most famously, Bainbridge was appointed to captain the *USS Constitution*, best known by its nickname, "Old Ironsides." At the helm of the *Constitution*, Bainbridge fought the British ship, *Java* in 1812, destroying and defeating the ship and earning his place as a naval legend. Constructed in 1797, during the final months of George Washington's presidency, the *Constitution* still graces the waters of Boston as the oldest naval vessel still afloat.[70]

While the life of a famous ship commander might sound glamorous, William Bainbridge was captured by foreign forces three different times during his career. The conditions of pris-

---

70   *USS Constitution* Museum, https://ussconstitutionmuseum.org/. Retrieved January 19, 2019.

ons of the day were often more dangerous than the wartime fighting. Bainbridge fully understood the meaning of perseverance, and the myopic focus of overcoming circumstances that is often required for success, and even for survival.

So by the time the city was created on December 22, 1829, the Bainbridge name already stood for excellence, achievement, and bravery. Since its beginning, the city has challenged its people by its name. Cultures around the world have always placed great importance on names, whether in Biblical times or more recently with Native American tribes. President John F. Kennedy described America's special role of protecting freedom in the world by explaining that many children in different nations were named after George Washington or Thomas Jefferson. In the 21st century, people more often pass down family names or endow children with the names of famous people.

So how has Bainbridge measured up to its original name? The past 190 years have brought great success for both the city and its people.

The movie industry in Hollywood reached a new milestone in 1935, with the release of the first full-color, full-length film, *Becky Sharp*. The film produced an Oscar (Academy Award) nomination for Miriam Hopkins, one of the giants of early Hollywood movies.

Hopkins began using her vast talents as a young child, in Bainbridge. She sang in the St. John's Episcopal Church choir, a natural place since her great-grandfather was a founder of the church and a former mayor of Bainbridge.

The star of Bainbridge has not one, but two stars on the Hollywood Walk of Fame, one for movies and one for television accomplishments. She played in 36 full-length movies in a career that spanned four decades.[71]

The glamorous actress wasn't the only source of creativity in Bainbridge, especially in the 1940s. With the outbreak of World War II, the town saw the construction of the Bainbridge Army Airfield to train the seemingly countless new airplane pilots needed for the war effort. During the war, the great American novelist J.S. Salinger was stationed in Bainbridge and composed some of his great short-stories there.

Around the time of the first World War, a traveling Vaudeville company from Bainbridge gave rise to a record-setting career in American sports. The Four Novelty Grahams featured the members of the Stribling family, with two parents and two children. In its early days, the show included a skit with the two Stribling kids wearing oversized boxing gloves and pretending to fight. As the eldest Stribling began to grow, the show featured the chance for any volunteers to take on the first-born child, Young Stribling, in a boxing match.[72]

Soon thereafter, Stribling toured the country as a fighter, setting many records in the early days of professional box-

71 *New Georgia Encyclopedia*, "Miriam Hopkins," https://www.georgiaency-clopedia.org/articles/arts-culture/miriam-hopkins-1902-1972. Retrieved February 20, 2019.
72 *New Georgia Encyclopedia*, "Young Stribling," https://www.georgiaency-clopedia.org/articles/sports-outdoor-recreation/young-stribling-1904-1933.

ing as a popular nationwide sport. He appeared in a whop-ping 285 fights in just 12 years, and set the then-record of 125 career knockouts. He was tragically killed at the age of 28 in a motorcycle accident.

With Hollywood movies and box rings featuring chil-dren of Bainbridge, the legacy of its namesake was continued in a grand way, but nothing would match the town's rabid sup-port and intensity in a different arena: the football field.

Through its history, the Bainbridge High School Bear-cats have lived up to their city's name with tough, hard-hitting, highly-competitive football teams and all-star players reaching for new heights.

In football, there are few greater heights than the annu-al draft of college players. Becoming the number-one pick in the draft is one of the greatest honors in American sports, and one Bainbridge native actually did it twice. Ken Rice became the first overall pick of both the NFL draft and the AFL draft in 1960.[73] Before his professional career, he starred at Auburn University, where he was a three-time All-American lineman and named to just about every honor for which he was eligi-ble.[74]

In 1982, the Bearcats heightened the standard of the Bainbridge name with their first state championship.

If anyone in the state of Georgia understood living up to a name in 1982, it was the Bainbridge quarterback Bobby Walden. He was nicknamed "Little Bobby" for good reason. His dad, Bobby, was a college football star at the University of Georgia, a member of the Georgia Sports Hall of Fame, a punt-er for the Minnesota Vikings Super Bowl teams, and a 17-year star in the National Football League. He was nicknamed "the big toe from Cairo"[75] for his punting ability and his hometown. After his professional football career, Walden and his wife set-tled in Bainbridge to raise their son, "Little Bobby."

Retrieved July 9, 2019.
73   Boyles, Bob. Guido, Paul. *The USA Today College Football Encyclopedia.* Skyhorse Publishing Inc. 2009. pp. 135.
74   Georgia Sports Hall of Fame, "Ken Rice," http://gshf.org/pdf_files/induct-ees/football/ken_rice.pdf. Retrieved July 9, 2019.
75   Smith, Loran, "Bobby Walden - Big Toe From Cairo," https://georgiadogs.com/news/2018/9/5/football-bobby-walden-big-toe-from-cairo.aspx. Re-trieved October 9, 2019.

Little Bobby rarely missed a game or even a team practice when his dad played. He understood the game, and he understood the pressure on a team to win. After his Bainbridge days, the younger Walden signed a scholarship to play quarterback for Auburn University.[76]

The 1982 season brought not only a championship, but great memories. The 1982 defense shut out Cairo, 7-0, topping off the classic performance with a goal-line stand at the game's dramatic end. Cairo had the ball, first-and-goal, at the Bainbridge one-yard line, but the Bearcats defense stiffened and denied Cairo a score on four consecutive plays.

The state championship game sported an equally thrilling 7-6 win over Gainesville. Joe Crine, the legendary longtime sportswriter for the *Post Searchlight*, described the moment that the championship was re-lived at the team's 30-year reunion:

"While the 1982 players and coaches were being introduced at midfield, the Bearcats video scoreboard showed the replay of their winning championship scoring drive in a 7-6 victory over Gainesville.

"Fullback Scott Carroll, a team captain, ran in for the winning touchdown from 5 yards out after Kenneth Howard recovered a fumble by Gainesville fullback Sammy Williams at the 5-yard-line. Carroll and Howard are both medical doctors.

"Defensive back Mark Willis kicked the winning extra point, then later knocked a Gainesville player out of bounds as he tried to run in for a two-point conversion, to preserve the victory."[77]

The team featured a host of other talented players, including three players named to the first-team of the *Atlanta Journal-Constitution* all-state team: running back Calvin Close, linebacker Jackie Wilson, and lineman Jimmy Holton. Close

76   Murphy, Mark, "Dye-gest: AU Quarterbacks Through the Years," *247Sports.com*, April 3, 2012. https://247sports.com/college/auburn/Article/ Dye-Gest-AU-Quarterbacks-Through-the-Years-104891796/. Retrieved October 13, 2019.
77   Crine, Joe, "State champions share stories," *The Post Searchlight*, October 23, 2012. https://www.thepostsearchlight.com/2012/10/23/state-champi-ons-share-stories/. Retrieved January 19, 2019.

starred as a running back at Tuskegee University after his Bearcats days.[78] Jimmy Holton later played for the University of Georgia Bulldogs.[79]

At Tuskegee, Calvin Close was joined by two teammates, running back (and defensive back) Tim Flanders and all-state linebacker Jackie Wilson.

Running back Scott Carroll and Guard Greg Inlow signed to play at Georgia Southwestern, which had recently started its football program. They played under former Bainbridge head coach Jimmy Hightower.

Phillip Bryant, a junior on the 1982 team, signed with Florida State and later transferred to Georgia Southwestern.

After becoming part of the Georgia Bulldogs team, Holton transferred to Florida State, but a paperwork issue prevented that from working out, and he played the remainder of his college ball at Valdosta State.[80]

The team won its state championship on December 11, 1982, precisely 36 years to the day before the Bearcats would play again for the state title in 2018. The 1982 team had to play a rematch against Mitchell County, a team that had soundly defeated Bainbridge during the regular season. In 2018, Bainbridge had to face Warner Robins for a playoff rematch, avenging its worst loss of the season.

Thankfully, the two teams have a thing in common; both won their state championship games and entered the annals of Georgia sports history.

1982 Bainbridge Bearcats
State Champions
Class GHS 1-AAA
Coaches:

78   Georgia Sports Hall of Fame, 1983 All-stars, https://ghsfha.org/forum/topic/2813-1983-all-stars/. Retrieved June 19, 2019.
79   *SicEmDawgs.com*, 1983 UAG Football Signees, https://www.sicemdawgs.com/1983-uga-football-signees/, https://www.sicemdawgs.com/1983-uga-football-signees/. Retrieved June 19, 2019.
80   Statistics on college football scholarships for the 1982 state champion Bainbridge team were provided courtesy of Chip Ariail, statistician for the Bainbridge High School football program.

Ralph Jones – Head coach
Sonny Smart – Defensive coordinator, linebackers
Larry Clark – Ends, outside linebackers
Pete Reeves – Defensive backs
Dick Griffin – Defensive tackles
Dwight Gray – Receivers
Steve Bench – Offensive line, strength
Don Hancock – Offensive coordinator, running backs
Carlton Gainous – Ninth grade, offensive staff

Players:

Jeffery Gainous – SE
Michael Stubbs – QB
Bobby Walden – QB
Kenneth Howard – DB
Patrick Clark – DB
Hank Holt – QB
Cedric Edwards – DB
Mark Willis – DB/K
Reginald Butler – TB
Tommy Nix – DB
Bobby Stubbs – SE
Tim Flanders – RB
Greg Malone – WB
Alphonso Weaver – DB
Shellie Fountain – DB
Frank Key – WB
Danny Cooper – DB
Calvin Close – RB
Phillip Bryant – WR/DB
David Harper – DT
Terry Heard – LB
Andy Belcher – LB
Lonnie Hughes – FB
Jerome Roddy – FB
Lamar Sweet – DB
Greg Waddell – P
George Tucker – DT
Ed Guy – DT
Kenneth Davis – DB/SE
Tony Shuman – DB

53

Robert Harris – DB
Scott Carroll – FB
Alan Skinner – WB
Brian Key – C
Cole Forsyth – C
Eddie Smith – LB
Wade Kirkland – OG
Joe Wright – LB
Daniel Knight – LB
Tommy Doss – LB
Jackie Wilson – OG
Kevin Marvin – OG
Eddie Sapp – OG
Jeff Durham – OG
Greg Inlow – OG
Derrick Biggles – LB
David Williams – C
Eugene Williams – DE
Dale Daniels – OT
Tony Harris – DE
Eric Duke – G
Vince Lapapa – OT
Mackel Cooper – DT
Calvin Gaines – DT
Jimmy Holton – OT
Todd Mills – TE
Calvin Mills – TE
Donald Cooper – TE
David Sykes – SE
Pell Thompson – DB

Managers:
Pat Moore,
Joey Kendrick,
Brad Ward

Cheerleaders:
Mia McDaniel, Paula Anderson, Debra Burney,
Jennifer Medlin, Dana Brock, Deanna Jones,
Shannon Key, Angie Hooper

The First Family
of Georgia Football

As a child, Kirby Smart's life changed forever when he moved with his family from Alabama to Georgia in 1982.

Thirty-three years later, Coach Kirby Smart again moved from Alabama to Georgia, and this time it was the future of Georgia that would change.

In his adult life, Kirby Smart has called Bainbridge his "heart and soul,"[81] and it all started with the magical fall of 1982.

With the first move, the child of Coach Sonny Smart was, for a short time, in foreign territory. He was now in Georgia Bulldog country, and there was no better time for that. It was, at least so far, the greatest era in the rich history of the Bulldogs. That fall, Kirby's first in the state, Georgia would play in

Coach Kirby Smart, leader of the Georgia Bulldogs and proud Bainbridge Bearcat.

the national championship game for the second time in three years. Herschel Walker, almost indisputably the greatest college football player in history, would win the Heisman Trophy as the premier player in the sport.

And that wasn't the only great team the young Kirby was rooting for. His dad, a future Hall-of-Famer, had just been hired as the defensive coordinator at Bainbridge High School, working with the then-Bearcats head football coach Ralph Jones. The fall of 1982 brought magical results for the young Kirby. Georgia won the SEC championship and played in the Sugar Bowl against Penn State, coming up just a bit short of another national title. Only one thing could surpass the classic Georgia Bulldogs season, and that would be a championship for his

81   WTXL Road Trip: Kirby Smart Making Bainbridge Proud, *WTXL.com*, https://www.wtxl.com/sports/wtxl-road-trip-kirby-smart-making-bainbridge-proud/article_2f898ec6-5609-11e6-9de8-a34367847d69.html. Retrieved January 19, 2019.

Coach Kirby Smart
by the numbers

4

In just four years as the head coach of the Georgia Bulldogs, the Bainbridge native has won four championships, with the 2017 SEC championships and three consecutive SEC Eastern Division titles.

0

Coach Smart never has Bainbridge far from his mind, texting Coach Jeff Littleton to congratulate him on every win and offering condolences after losses. In his text after the state championship win, Smart admitted to Littleton that he was a little worried at the end of the fourth quarter.

2

Kirby Smart is the second Coach Smart to achieve great success in the rich tradition of Bainbridge football. His dad, the original Coach Smart, served as defensive coordinator for the 1982 state championship Bainbridge Bearcats.

6

Kirby Smart has won an amazing six national championships as an assistant coach. In only this third year as head coach, Smart took the Georgia Bulldogs to within an overtime period of his seventh.

daddy's team, the Bainbridge Bearcats.

Sure enough, in this incomparable year for the young Kirby, he had the thrill of watching the Bainbridge Bearcats, propelled in no small part by his dad's defense, capture the school's first state championship. To make things even better, the championship game was won largely on defense, a 7-6 thriller of a final score, with a defensive stop of a two-point conversion attempt by the Gainesville offense.

At that young age, Kirby had already decided that he wanted to win games with his dad at Bainbridge, and that he wanted to play football for the University of Georgia.[82]

It's easy for the media and less-than-industrious writers to spout cliches about how Kirby Smart was the son of a coach who excelled solely on his knowledge of the game against superior athletes at the college level. While it's true that he was maybe undersized for a safety in the Southeastern Conference, he was nonetheless an outstanding athlete who excelled at both the high school and college levels.

By the fall of 1993, Sonny Smart was the head coach at Bainbridge, and his son Kirby had grown into a team leader and all-state performer. The Bearcats made another playoff run, this time advancing to the state's final four.

In his first college game, he had a whopping three quarterback sacks on South Carolina's Steve Taneyhill. His life as a Georgia Bulldog had truly begun. In two games against the future NFL number-one draft pick Tim Couch, Kirby intercepted the star quarterback three different times.[83]

Despite the talent and the well-documented competitiveness that have marked his career, Kirby Smart has become an elite coach and recruiter because he has lived according to timeless advice: remember who you are.

"That's the thing about Kirby; he hasn't changed at all," explained Brian Hill, co-defensive coordinator at Bainbridge High School. Hill actually met Smart at Valdosta State University, where Smart was an assistant coach and Hill was pur-

82   Hummer, Steve, "From his home school to his hometown, Smart has them amped," *Atlanta Journal-Constitution*, August 26, 2016. https://www.ajc.com/sports/college/from-his-home-school-his-hometown-smart-has-them-amped/6gHWi3GvbAv1c0ITjXXixN/#. Retrieved June 19, 2019.

83   Id.

suing his graduate degree. They were flag football teammates and part of the same group of friends.

"That's why he's such a great recruiter," Hill added. "He's real, and you know who he is."[84]

"We saw him on the little league fields and the midget football fields," Former Bainbridge High School Principal Tommie Howell said to the RedandBlack.com, "We watched him grow up. He's one of our children."[85]

After marrying a former Georgia Bulldogs basketball player, Mary Beth Lycett, Smart worked as a young coach at a few different schools before landing at Louisiana State University with Coach Nick Saban. At the University of Alabama, Saban and Smart teamed together for national championships in 2009, 2011, 2012, and 2015.

Then, Kirby came home.

84   Brian Hill (Bainbridge defensive football coach) in discussion with the author, November 23, 2019.
85   Alexander, Wilson, "The evolution of Kirby Smart: How a boy from Bainbridge became the head coach at UGA," *The Red and Black*, August 25, 2016. https://www.redandblack.com/sports/the-evolution-of-kirby-smart-how-a-boy-from-bainbridge/article_325eb364-6a5a-11e6-b652-fbd04355b6cb.html. Retrieved September 27, 2019.

This time, the move from Alabama to Georgia came with slightly more publicity than the Smarts' move in 1982, and this time it was the University of Georgia's future that quickly changed. In just his third season at the helm of his alma mater's team, Smart led Georgia to the SEC championship and an overtime epic thriller of a national championship game that came up just slightly short against the team Smart had left to come to Georgia. Smart's defense had shut out Alabama in the national championship game's opening half, and only the unveiling of one of the game's great legends, then-freshman Tua Tagovailoa, prevented Georgia's national championship run.

But that was merely one game, and under the leadership of the Bainbridge High School alumnus, Georgia has remained an elite football program and one of the top championship contenders each year. As of this book's publication, Smart's teams have now won the SEC East for the third year in a row.

After the storm

So as the Bainbridge Bearcats players found themselves in the middle of a hurricane-induced disruption of their hometown and school, they still had something to aspire to: a name. The name Bainbridge still meant achievement. The name still meant courage. Maybe most importantly, the Bainbridge name meant overcoming adversity.

Overcoming adversity, as people inevitably learn, often requires careful planning. So does caring for scores of young men who may or may not have food at their homes. On the Sunday after the hurricane, Coach Littleton called Mark and Connie Mitchell. As the current and past presidents of the Bearcat Touchdown Club, they were the ones Littleton could turn to for an extremely important request.

"On Sunday afternoon after Hurricane Michael devastated our community, Coach Littleton called and asked us if there was any way that we could provide meals for the team the upcoming week as the team prepared to play Warner Robins," the Mitchells recalled. "Fortunately, we were in Columbus, GA when Coach Lit called, so we were able to stock up on what was needed and bring everything back to Bainbridge. We cooked one or more meals each day to serve the team after practice concluded. We were able to send food home to those who had little to no food, or a way to prepare any food without electricity."[86]

The work by the Bearcats Touchdown Club was not lost on the school or the community. "The Touchdown Club did a phenomenal job with helping the coaches and the team," explained Roy Mathews, principal of Bainbridge High School. "Even in normal times they have done so much to empower our team to rise to the next level of success."[87]

So while the Touchdown Club prepared meals and helped in many ways, and while the school prepared to help their student body, Littleton and his staff began preparing for the both storm relief and the rest of the season. The preparation also included regular meetings with the principal. "Coach Littleton met with me pretty often in the days and weeks after the hurricane. I was kept up to date on who needed what, and how the players and their families were doing. Coach let me know how we could help the team and I supported them in whatever ways were necessary," recalled Roy Mathews, the principal of Bainbridge.[88] As a former coach at Bainbridge, the second-year-principal understood the needs of the athletic department and the desire to help players and their families.

Mathews was also busy doing much of the same work on a school-wide scale, checking on teachers, students, staff, and families. Working through efforts to help those in need became just one more part of the job.

The team certainly didn't have to wonder whether the coaches had their backs when it counted. For all the talk about tough times and adversity, they were living it in real time. The coaches were checking on them and their families. The coaches arranged for a generator to produce electricity so players could bathe. The coaches arranged meals for the players and many families.

86   Mark and Connie Mitchell (Bearcats Touchdown Club presidents) in discussion with the author, December 16, 2019.
87   Roy Mathews (Bainbridge High School principal) in discussion with the author, December 14, 2019.
88   Id.

The great comeback of 2018 required each component part of the team to work together as one unit. The offense, which brought a mixture of experience and youth into the season, ultimately became a group making big plays at big times.
(Photo courtesy of Elizabeth P. Hill).

They may not have been facing enemy capture and time as a prisoner of war like William Bainbridge did three different times, but they could still live up to the standards of his name.

All of that sounded good, but most of the season was over and the Bainbridge Bearcats still had a losing record. There was now no margin for error. A single loss would likely mean the end of their dreams of that season,

They had to win every game. There was no backup plan.

Chapter 4

The Comeback

> "I have nothing to offer but blood, toil, tears and sweat.... You ask, what is our aim? I can answer in one word: It is victory...."
>
> --Winston Churchill

For most football teams, the first and second halves of the season are divided by the number of games played. For the typical ten-game schedule, that would mean that the first half of the season was the first five games.

For the Bainbridge Bearcats and the other teams whose communities lay in the path of Hurricane Michael, the other logical divider would be the seven games before the massive storm, and the remaining games afterward.

But not Bainbridge.

It might not make mathematical sense, but the 2018 season was divided by the first eight games, and then the remainder of the season.

The season was divided not by the names on the schedule, but within the hearts, spirits, and souls of the players.

In the weeks after the hurricane, there was little normalcy in Bainbridge. Some students came to school without the benefit of electricity at home to provide light for homework and studying. Others were displaced from the solace of their bedrooms by holes in their home's roof. Asking almost any teenager, or thinking back to one's own youth, about the importance of one's bedroom or wherever their place is for time alone, and the impact of that will become clear.

For many, there was no family dinner table for dinner or time with parents. Television wasn't available, nor was the internet in many areas.

Cars were damaged, some beyond repair. Indoor

plumbing was an issue for some with extensive home damage.

So for the kids of the Bainbridge football team, the first opponent after the storm wasn't a football team at all; it was normalcy itself. Sure, they wanted to win, but most of all they wanted to win their old lives back.

That was not all they wanted. They also wanted to help. After practices, Michael Ryan would give rides home to teammates without transportation. Before returning home, he would first drive to help in areas of Bainbridge where trees were being sawed to remove them from homes, cars, or driveways. So after a full-speed football practice, helping the team lift crates of food or bottled water for the community, giving rides home, and sawing trees for people, he would finally return home and help care for his dad, who was battling cancer and recovering from treatments.

"We were so proud of everything he was doing, and we were watching him grow up when his teammates and community needed him," Jeremy Ryan recalled.

As their world had figuratively turned upside down the football team was literally maturing before the eyes of their coaches and community. As for football, it remained as uncertain as the city's recovery from the storm. The team's won-loss record was not good, and they hardly had time to prepare for the upcoming road game. Like the hurricane, the first half of the season had been something that everyone would like to forget. Neither was possible, so all the guys could do was try to recover and rebuild after both.

Coach Randy Hill knows something about pulling together and having each other's backs. In the jungles of Vietnam, Hill earned a Silver Star for bravery under fire when he risked his life to save a fallen fellow soldier. He ran, literally under heavy gunfire, and pulled the wounded colleague to safety. The man was not Hill's best friend, or a close friend, or even someone whose name he knew. He was a fellow soldier, and that was all that mattered. The same selfless spirit that made him a hero is also the reason that he deflects when asked about his bravery. So when Coach Hill said he saw the team begin to come together after the hurricane and under the leadership of their coaches, he speaks with the voice of experience.

Little did the players and coaches know it, but the first half of the season would not end until the final seconds of the fourth quarter in this, the eighth game of the year. Nor could they have ever imagined that the hurricane was only the first of the highly-charged events that would make this a historic season.

So with the challenge of regaining normalcy, and with the seemingly endless distractions, the last thing they needed was a highly-regarded team to play in their first post-storm game.

Enter Warner Robins.

Bainbridge vs. Warner Robins
October 19, 2018

The game turned out great, at least during halftime. That was the special moment when Roy Mathews, the principal at Bainbridge High School, met the Warner Robins principal on the field. Warner Robins presented a donation of over $2,000 to the hurricane relief efforts of the Bainbridge schools. The home team had taken up money at the gate by entering Warner Robins fans and presented the proceeds. "That went a long way with me," Mathews recalled. "That was a thoughtful and helpful gesture. We placed the funds in an account operated by the school system and were able to help people who really needed it."

So halftime was a win for Bainbridge. On the field? Not so much. There could not have been a worse team for the Bainbridge Bearcats to face in their first game as a hurricane-ravaged school and community.

On paper, given the circumstances facing Bainbridge, the game seemed like a mismatch. Only months later, in a television interview, did a true glimpse of the night come from Bainbridge head coach Jeff Littleton.

But that would come later. On this night, the result might have seemed inevitable.

Warner Robins stood tall as one of the elite names in

Emerging from the fog, the 2018 Bainbridge Bearcats storm the field, led by number 30, Roman Harrison. Harrison was named Class AAAAA Defensive Player of the Year. Harrison signed a football scholarship with the University of Tennessee, where he contributed greatly as a freshman. (Photo courtesy of Elizabeth P. Hill).

American high school football. The school has won multiple national championships and multiple state championships.

Warner Robins High School has placed its alumni in the NFL, Major League Baseball, championship college football teams, the Georgia governor's mansion, the cabinet of the President of the United States, the red carpet television and movie awards ceremonies, and at a high level in the Pentagon.

Even the name, Warner Robins, arises from a true winner. The first commander of the then-Wellston Air Force Depot, Colonel Charles Thomas, wanted to re-name the base after the legendary General A. Warner Robins. The problem, according to Air Force regulations, was that the base had to be named after the nearest town.

With a typical can-do attitude that preceded modern government bureaucracy, Colonel Thomas worked and persuaded the nearby town of Wellston to change its name to Warner Robins, Georgia.[89]

That attitude has marked the success of the U. S. Air Force base, the city, and the high school that bear the general's name today.

So, with their community in disarray, and with the seemingly best of Georgia high school football standing on the opposite sideline, Bainbridge charged into battle.

The result was, of course, predictable. Warner Robins won their home game against the impaired opponent by the final score of 38-0. They dominated the total yardage 398 to 79. Bainbridge was zero-for-11 in third-down conversions, while Warner Robins was 7-for-14.[90]

What was not predictable, however, was the conclusion of the game. Even late in the game, with a blowout victory well in hand, the Demons ran passing plays to run up the score. Astonishingly, they called an onside kick after a late score. Comments were unnecessary; the events spoke for themselves.

The final score was a wipeout, but in some ways the result, surprisingly, was not.

Quietly, Bearcats head coach Jeff Littleton knew that he and his coaching staff had devised a winning game plan for the game. He knew, as an adult, that the circumstances of the day were just too traumatic for a young team to overcome in a few days for a road game at Warner Robins.

"We spent much more time taking care of the kids and making sure their families were alright than we did preparing for a football game," recalled Coach Joe Dollar. "We did our jobs and prepared, but many of the players weren't there for practices, and our big concern was to be there for them in whatever way they needed us. The football game was secondary."[91]

What Littleton knew, however, was something he and

89   Dixon, Claire (1993). *Warner Robins: The Second 25 Years.* Alpharetta, GA: WH Wolfe Associates.
90   Game statistics provided by the Bainbridge High School Bearcats coaching staff, and specifically by statistician Chip Ariail.
91   Joe Dollar (Bainbridge defensive football coach) in discussion with the

his coaches would later hold as a closely guarded secret. After watching the score inflated against his team, Littleton and the entire organization wanted a rematch. If Bainbridge were to somehow make the playoffs, which wasn't yet impossible, they aspired to face the mighty Warner Robins Demons again.

Despite the 38-0 blowout, despite the less-than-100 yards of offense, and despite the miserable final game stats, Littleton knew the offensive game plan was in place.

If they got the rematch, the offensive game plan would remain unchanged.

Bainbridge vs. Harris County
October 26, 2018

The end of October would bring both a win and a loss. Although its destruction still plagued the community, Hurricane Michael now stood in the rear-view mirror, even if only by a few weeks.

After the Warner-Robins loss, the Bainbridge coaches and team saw what could happen when a group loses focus on its ultimate objective.

The next opponent was Harris County, from Hamilton, Georgia.

This was one of those games where the final score of 49-0 did not reflect the margin between the two teams.

Actually, it was much worse.

After running up a 35-0 halftime lead, Bainbridge mercifully scored only two second-half touchdowns.[92]

The only question was whether the offense or the defense dominated more. For the entire game, the Bearcats defense surrendered on two first-downs.

In one of the most amazing stats you might ever see in an athletic contest, Harris County managed a total of 14 yards of total offense for the game. Their running attack gained 16 yards on 17 plays, and their passing game had negative-two yards for the game.

---

author, December 16, 2019.
92   Game statistics provided by the Bainbridge High School Bearcats coaching staff, and specifically by statistician Chip Ariail.

Anthony Brooks led the defense with nine tackles (seven unassisted) and Randy Fillingame had seven tackles (six unassisted).

The offense was equally lethal against Harris County. Caleb McDowell had 14 carries for a jaw-dropping 174 yards, averaging 12.4 yards each time he carried the ball. Rashad Broadnax had 17 rushes for 76 yards, and Tevin McCray added 68 yards on only eight carries.[93]

Quayde Hawkins lit up the Harris County defense with the aerial attack, completing 77-percent of his passes (10-of-13) for three touchdowns and 116 yards. Aaron Spivie, Adrian Cooper, and Deyon Bouie each caught touchdown passes, with Spivie leading the yardage with 58 yards on five catches.[94]

The victory put the Bainbridge record at four wins and five losses after nine games. Despite everything, their ultimate goals remained possible. The Bearcats still stood alive in the hunt for the playoffs.

No More

Equally impressive was the fact that the playoffs weren't the only thing still alive in the Bainbridge locker room. The players still held out hope. Part of that hope lay in their leaders, the coaches, who had taught them, prepared them, mentored them, and challenged them. Just three seasons earlier, Bainbridge had blown through its schedule to a 13-1 record and a spot in the Final 4 of the Class AAAAA playoffs. Their only loss was to the Cartersville team featuring future Clemson quarterback Trevor Lawrence, who threw two touchdown passes to future Alabama tight end Miller Forristall. Coach Jeff Littleton had been named the 2015 Class AAAAA Atlanta Falcons Coach of the Year, and the current players either played on that team or remembered it well.

Their hope also lay in themselves as competitors and as personal achievers. "It was during that game week that the team began coming together in a deeper way," recalled Coach Brian Hill. Others agreed. "I think that's when the struggles of

---

93 Id.
94 Id.

dealing with the hurricane and the disappointing season up to that point came to a head, and the players said, 'No more,'" said Powell Cobb of the *Post Searchlight*. "When Bainbridge convincingly beat Harris County and Thomas County Central those next two weeks, you could tell this was a different team. They were playing for each other and for a community desperate for something positive to happen, and that's a hell of a recipe."

Caleb's mom

Just when things seemingly could not get worse, they did.

One of the saddest effects of catastrophes like Hurricane Michael is that they often force children and teenagers to deal with adult issues at a tender age. Parents usually aspire to let their kids be kids as long as possible, with varying results depending on family circumstances.

Tragically, the loss to Warner Robins was painful and sad, but it was nothing compared to another, much greater loss before the month ended.

About 11 months after the 1982 Bainbridge state championship in football, Andre and Kimberly Conner welcomed their first child into the world. Latorya Conner was an exemplary young girl, and became an honors graduate of Bainbridge High School. She earned multiple degrees in Early Childhood Education, including the Educational Specialist degree.

On October 29, 2018, the world lost Latorya Conner way too soon.[95]

She loved her parents, grandparents, siblings, three God-parents, God-siblings, and extended family. She had a mother's unique love for her two sons, Caleb and Corey McDowell.

So, on the heels of watching mother nature's demolition of much of their community, the boys of Bainbridge now had to experience their friend and teammate's unspeakable pain and grief.

---

95   Latorya Coller, Bruton Morturary, https://www.tributearchive.com/obituaries/3404655/Latorya-Conner. Retrieved January 19, 2019.

As the 2018 season progressed, so did the play and leadership of sophomore quarterback Quayde Hawkins (wearing jersey #1). Tough times are common for rookie quarterbacks, but the coaching staff had the discernment to see his development and encourage him in ways that helped him lead the team to the state championship. Photo courtesy of Elizabeth P. Hill.

Caleb McDowell now had to continue his studies at school, be a brother to Corey, deal with the countless life changes from the hurricane, and grieve the loss of his mom.

Life was imposing too much pain on these kids.

This was the point where leadership became more important than ever before. Jeff Littleton and his coaches now were coaches, tutors, mentors, grief counselors, and family. The coaches visited Caleb and his dad, Derik. Rev. Brooks, the team chaplain also connected with Derik, whom he had known for many years, to reach out for prayer, conversation, offering to spend time whenever needed, and checking on them.

The stakes were now much higher than football. The hurricane, passing of Caleb's mom, and cancer diagnosis of

Jeremy Ryan had changed the dynamics of lives and entire families.

The team depended on their leader. For the rest of their lives, the kids would remember how they were led after this. They might or might not remember their overall record, or many of the individual games, but they would remember how their coaches reacted to real adversity. They would remember how the coaches dealt with the hurricane and its aftermath. They would remember how the coaches helped Caleb deal with the loss of his mom.

In this season of complete uncertainty, that was the one thing that was absolutely certain.

They would remember. They would remember this when they lost jobs, or marriages, or family members in the future. They would remember this during their darkest hours.

They would remember.

No matter where his career path might ultimately lay, this just might become Littleton's biggest challenge.

The coaches transformed football from an extracurricular activity to an anchor. In many ways, football became even more important than ever. For many of the players, football became the oasis of stability in a life of upheaval. It became

72

Images

from the 2018 Bainbridge playoff run

(Above) The majorettes of the Bainbridge High School band perform at halftime of the state championship game, adding pageantry to the event. (Below) The Bainbridge players walk through the victory line at the send-off for the state championship game.

(Above) The Bearcats cheerleaders did an outstanding job with the large crowd that made the Atlanta trip to support their team. (Below) Thousands of Bainbridge fans made plenty of noise at the state championship game. (Right) The fans came prepared to help.

(Above) Coaches' wives, led by Kristi Littleton (center) and Margie Hill (center left) helped the fans maintain their "12th man" advantage with over 5,000 supporting the Bearcats. (Below) Coach Brian Hill and wife (and photographer) Liz enjoy championship day with daughters Aubrey (15), Addison (12), and Alden (8).

the constant, daily connection to their normalcy. Football became their way to join a greater cause, beyond their own lives, of teaming together to rise above circumstances.

One game remained. Amazingly, because they had performed well in region games, the playoffs stood within their reach.

Nine of their ten games were behind them. They sported a losing record, but the opportunity for a comeback lay within their grasp. If their entire community could come together, why couldn't they?

The distractions were mounting. The grief was an unavoidable presence, first for Caleb's loss, for the damaged community, and for normalcy.

With one game remaining, it was time to focus the energies of an entire group on one goal.

It was time for a place in the playoffs, if they could earn it.

It was time for a new second-half of the season, if they could earn it.

Bainbridge vs. Thomas County Central
November 2, 2018

The season finale brought a season-defining game for both teams.

For the Thomas County Central Yellowjackets, whose record stood at 5-4, the game would determine whether another winning season would be added to the annals of an elite tradition.

The 2018 season also marked the 25th anniversary of a feat that stood alone in Georgia's rich football history, when the school produced both the 1993 state champs in football, the national championship quarterback in college football, and the 1993 Heisman Trophy winner, alumnus Charlie Ward of Florida State University. Ward, who later played basketball in the NBA, won the football national championship for the Seminoles that year.

So there was much on the line for the winner of the season's final contest.

For much of the first quarter, the game was close. Bainbridge struck first, with a six-play, 53-yard scoring drive that ended with a 24-yard, Quayde Hawkins-to-Aaron Spivie aerial connection for a touchdown. Hawkins would connect on nine-of-14 passes for an impressive 223 yards[96]. After a Yellowjacket field goal, the game remained tight and suspenseful.

And then, with one pass, everything changed.

One of the great expressions in sports is that "chicks dig the long ball," meaning that the way to impress the girls is through the big home run, the long, three-point shot in basketball, the 300-yard drive in golf, and the long touchdown.

The season finale definitely brought out the long ball in the Bainbridge arsenal.

A 45-yard strike from Hawkins to Rashad Broadnax made it a 14-3 game, and the Bearcats had begun their demolition of Thomas County Central. For the night, Broadnax had two catches but he made them count. He turned both of his receptions into touchdowns, with a total of 61 yards.

Adrian Cooper joined in the aerial assault, hauling in two catches for a whopping 80 yards and a touchdown. Deyon Bouie had one catch, for 38 yards, and Caleb McDowell had a catch for 16 yards along with his team-leading 71 rushing yards that included his own long ball, a 46-yard touchdown run.[97]

Overall, the Bearcats exploded for 37 unanswered points to put the game far out of reach before the Yellowjackets put up a meaningless touchdown with a minute remaining in the game.

For the second game in a row, the Bearcats defense held the opponents to a single-digit number of first downs. For the second game in a row, the defense held the opponent to less than a hundred yards in both passing and rushing offense. The Bearcats "D" stifled the Yellowjackets, holding them to a paltry 1-for-11 on third-down conversions.

Randy Fillingame continued his elite senior season with 12 tackles (with an impressive ten unassisted), three sacks, and a dominant six tackles-for-loss. Anthony Brooks also dominated with five of his seven tackles going for lost yardage. Spivie

---

96   Game statistics provided by the Bainbridge High School Bearcats coaching staff, and specifically by statistician Chip Ariail.
97   Id.

added a 54-yard pick-six interception return for a touchdown, his second of the game.

The final score of the game was 44-11.[98]

The final regular season record was now rendered meaningless, because the final score of the season was not a number but instead a word: playoffs.

The great William Faulkner, at his estate in Oxford, Mississippi, once wrote about a community that the past was not only forgotten; it wasn't even in the past.[99] For the Bainbridge Bearcats, the opposite was true. The past, at least in terms of football, was gladly forgotten. The past, in terms of the ravaging storm, would gladly be placed in the rear-view mirror. The past, the suffering of a community, could gladly be suspended for a time while the community rallied around its young heroes who seized a playoff berth from the jaws of disaster, adversity, and grief.

The second season now lay ahead. The first season was

---

98   Id.
99   Faulkner, William, *Requiem for a Nun*, Penguin Random House (1951).

about football, and the second season would be about coming together as a family.

They would now enter the playoffs against some of the biggest names in Georgia high school football.

Their hometown might be small, but their dreams stood as tall as those of anyone else.

Chapter 5

The Playoffs

"For me, winning isn't something that happens suddenly on the field when the whistle blows and the crowds roar. Winning is something that builds physically and mentally every day that you train and every night that you dream."
- Emmit Smith

So the Bainbridge Bearcats barely made it to the play-offs, but their odds of long-range success weren't exactly great. Their 5-5 record made them a prohibitive underdog for the postseason run. In most sports playoffs, the top-seed-ed teams are rewarded for an outstanding season with first-round matchups against the weakest teams. For Bainbridge, with a relatively weak won-loss record, that meant a first-round matchup against 8-2 Jones County.

The State Playoffs
The Opening Round
Bainbridge vs. Jones County
November 9, 2018

The Greyhounds blew through their schedule, outscor-ing their regular season opponents by over a 2-to-1 margin. They won eight of their first nine games before dropping a cliffhanger, 17-10 road game at Stockbridge, one of the state's best teams. Only one of their wins was by seven points or less, and that was the season opener on the road.

In short, the game looked like a mismatch on paper.

Thankfully the games are not played on paper, with computers, or in the minds of the media experts. While the media unknowingly predicted doom for the 5-5 Bearcats, the Bainbridge coaches knew that things weren't so simple. The freshmen and sophomores had begun to mature as the season progressed. After the hurricane, the team had developed a togetherness that began to manifest in stronger performances.

"That's the number-one thing that Coach Littleton did;

Jackson Wheeler became an outstanding tight end, making him an important part of both the receivers and the offensive line. Although originally a competitor for the quarterback position, he was a team player who worked hard at the position that would best help the team achieve their aspirations for a state championship. (Photo courtesy of Elizabeth P. Hill).

he led the team and he held it together after the storm," explained co-defensive coordinator Brian Hill. "When many teams would have given up, after the losing record and the distractions of the hurricane, Jeff led as a head coach, and he and the staff teamed together to turn a challenge into an opportunity."[100]

While togetherness is great, Bainbridge still had to face the impressive 8-2 Jones County opponent. And that's exactly how the game began. On its second possession of the game, the Greyhounds completed a 45-yard touchdown pass with eight minutes remaining in the first quarter. Less than three

100   Brian Hill (Bainbridge defensive football coach) in discussion with the author, November 23, 2019.

minutes later, Jones County struck again with a thirty-yard field goal to seize a 10-0 lead with 5:34 remaining in the opening quarter of play.

Then, just 20 seconds later, Bainbridge began its run to glory. What followed in the next three-and-a-half quarters was described by Macon, Georgia's newspaper, *The Telegraph*, as "arguably the most shocking results from the first round of the playoffs." *The Telegraph* article described the rest of the game artfully: "The surprising part is the fashion in which it beat Jones County. Bainbridge got down early but didn't give up. It stormed back to take the lead and never let it go."[101]

The scoring onslaught by Bainbridge began a mere 20 seconds after the Jones County field goal, when Rashad Broadnax scored on a touchdown run that made it 10-7.

In the opening moments of the second quarter, Bainbridge seized the lead with a 13-play, 75-yard scoring drive capped with a Caleb McDowell touchdown run of 11 yards. Five minutes later, Aaron Spivie ran for a 24-yard touchdown score and the rout was on.

After falling behind 10-0, Bainbridge unleashed a 40-3 scoring run for the remainder of the game. Bainbridge racked up 21 first downs while holding the Greyhounds to a paltry six for the entire night. Jones County managed negative-eight yards rushing for the game, and converted just one of 12 third-downs.

Caleb McDowell, emerging as the truly talented back that the coaches had expected, ran for 116 yards and three touchdowns while averaging almost five yards-per carry. Aaron Spivie, Rashad Broadnax, and quarterback Quayde Hawkins each contributed rushing touchdowns. Hawkins also added 116 yards passing, including a 42-yard strike to Deyon Bouie.[102]

Senior star Roman Harrison led the way with ten tackles, including three tackles-for-loss. Because Jones County only

101   Baxley, Justin, Middle Georgia high school football scores, highlights: Upsets headline first round of playoffs, *The Telegraph*, November 10, 2019. https://www.macon.com/sports/high-school/article221408745.html. Retrieved July 9, 2019.
102   Game statistics provided by the Bainbridge High School Bearcats coaching staff, and specifically by statistician Chip Ariail.

ran 48 plays (compared to 75 by Bainbridge), there weren't as many tackles to make so the individual totals were lower than one would typically see. The defensive backfield didn't let that interfere with their making big plays. Deyon Bouie intercepted two passes, and Jaylen Peterson and Fred Thompson each picked off a pass.

Aaron Spivie dominated the special teams, with an 81-yard kickoff return highlighting his three kickoff returns for 119 yards and one punt return for 28 yards.[103]

By the end of the game, the growing power of the Bainbridge team, in all three phases of the game, had become clear. As sportswriter Justin Baxley of *The Telegraph* opined, "Bainbridge has the ability now to shock some others if it plays the way it did against Jones County."[104]

The State Playoffs
The Second Round
Bainbridge vs. Wayne County
November 16, 2018

If the first-round playoff matchup seemed daunting, the second-round clash brought the undefeated Wayne County High School. The Yellow Jackets sported not only an undefeated record of 11-0, but brought a roster loaded with future college prospects. No less than ten of their seniors signed college scholarships,[105] and along with underclassmen who will ultimately play at the next level, the Yellow Jackets roster made the undefeated season easy to understand.

One of those future college players, running back Ashby Cribb, started the scoring with a three-yard touchdown run from the wildcat formation. It would be the first of his two scores. Cribb also rushed for over 100 yards and averaged

103   Id.
104   Baxley, Justin, Middle Georgia high school football scores, highlights: Upsets headline first round of playoffs, *The Telegraph*, November 10, 2019. https://www.macon.com/sports/high-school/article221408745.html. Retrieved July 9, 2019.
105   Sulkowski, Frank, Complete National Signing Day Recap from WJCL 22 News, WJCL 22, February 6, 2019. https://www.wjcl.com/article/complete-national-signing-day-recap-from-wjcl-22-news/26230428. Retrieved November 22, 2019.

almost 40 yards per punt for the game.

Bainbridge might have still been a young team bio-logically, but their experience on and off the field had trans-formed them into a veteran team that now added composure to their talent. Facing an early deficit, the Bearcats immedi-ately marched on an 11-play, 73-yard scoring drive that sent a clear message to their senior-laden opponent. Quarterback Quayde Hawkins scored on a one-yard run, the first of the two touchdowns he provided. Late in the third quarter, Hawkins added an aerial touchdown with a pass to Adrian Cooper to give Bainbridge its first lead of the game at 13-12 with 1:48 remaining in the period.

In the fourth quarter, the Caleb McDowell show began. Wayne County had started an early fourth-quarter drive that ended abruptly at the 30-yard line when McDowell picked off a Yellow Jackets pass and darted into the end zone for a pick-six and a broadened lead.

Just two minutes later, McDowell matched his defensive touchdown with a score from the offensive side. His 77-yard run put Bainbridge up by two touchdowns and gave the Bear-cats all the scoring they needed for the second-round upset victory. Wayne County scored again just 95 seconds after Mc-Dowell's run, but the Bearcats impressive defense kept them out of the end zone for the remainder of the game.

That was not all the Bainbridge defense did. In the last two games, the Bearcats faced two high-octane offenses of teams with a combined record of 20 wins and only one loss between them. In those two games the Bainbridge defense forced a whopping ten turnovers, five in each game, includ-ing the pick-six that broke open the one-point game against Wayne County.

Once again, Roman Harrison led the team in tackles, with seven, and with tackles-for-loss with three. Bryce Worthy and Anthony Brooks each added six tackles and a tackle for loss. The Bearcats intercepted three Wayne County passes, two by Caleb McDowell and one by Deyon Bouie.

The offense was led by the outstanding aerial attack launched with the arm of quarterback Quayde Hawkins. Orig-inally the source of a multi-candidate competition during summer practice, the decision of head coach Jeff Littleton to go with the sophomore Hawkins was paying large dividends in the postseason. Hawkins passed for 237 yards with no interceptions. Adrian Cooper caught three passes for 88 yards and a touchdown, while fellow receiver Aaron Spivie hauled in six catches for 84 yards. Not surprisingly, Caleb McDowell led the ground attack with 111 yards on 20 carries.[106]

Bainbridge, amazingly, was now headed for the state playoff quarterfinals. Finally, on the 16th of November, in the second round of the playoffs, Bainbridge had clinched a winning record for the season. That fact served as just one more reminder of how far the Bainbridge team had traveled in its maturity and success. The name Bainbridge was surfacing in media reports and playoff predictions across the state of Georgia.

It was another name, however, that had captured the imagination of the players and coaches alike. It was a name to which head coach Jeff Littleton took an unusual approach as the game week practices progressed before the quarterfinal playoff round.

The next opponent, however, could wait a day or so. The Bainbridge Bearcats had just pulled off one of the year's greatest upsets. They were headed for the Elite Eight of the Class AAAAA playoffs.

---

106   Game statistics provided by the Bainbridge High School Bearcats coaching staff, and specifically by statistician Chip Ariail.

Chapter 6

The Run to Glory

"I'll do whatever it takes to win games, whether it's sitting on a bench waving a towel, handing a cup of water to a teammate, or hitting the game-winning shot."

- Kobe Bryant

The State Playoffs
The Elite Eight Round
"The Green Team"
Bainbridge vs. Buford
November 23, 2018

They were known, simply, as "the green team." At least that's what head coach Jeff Littleton called the Buford Wolves in the week leading up to the state playoff quarterfinals clash between Bainbridge and "the green team."[107]

Littleton's idea gave the coaching staff a way to name their opponent without speaking the name that has become an intimidating force in high school football. Littleton fully understood the power of names in sports, as some names carry the power to intimidate. South Carolina head football coach Will Muschamp expressed that idea well, before his team's 2019 game against Alabama, saying that the first goal was not to lose the game to the name of Alabama before his team took the field.

Littleton also understood that his roster, loaded with young players, carried the potential to become distracted by the big stage and the opponent's big name. Buford has won at an elite level for many years, totaling 11 state championships and an almost countless number of region titles. On national signing day, the 2018 Buford team had no less than 17 seniors sign college football scholarships. That represents almost all of their starters on both sides of the ball, but does not count

107   Jeff Littleton (Bainbridge head football coach) in discussion with the author, December 3, 2019.

the many players in the junior class who were also future college players. In just a few months, those 17 Buford seniors
would become players on the rosters of universities such as
Georgia, Ole Miss, LSU, Florida, Texas, Ohio State, Duke, Miami, West Georgia, Kennesaw State, Coastal Carolina, Wofford,
Tennessee Tech, Berry, and Lenoir-Rhyne.[108] A visit to rivals.
com reveals many Buford players listed among the most highly
recruited players in Georgia for both the 2019 and 2020 class-
es.[109]

    For Bainbridge, that meant that facing Buford meant al-

---

108   *GwinnettPrepSports.com*, "2019 Gwinnett County Football Signees
By High School," February 6, 2019. https://www.gwinnettprepsports.com/
schools/peachtree_ridge/gwinnett-county-football-signees-by-high-school/
article_7718af16-2a81-11e9-8575-970efb13f63a.html. Retrieved November
26, 2019.
109   Rivals.com, "2020 Rivals.com Georgia Top 100," https://n.rivals.com/

most facing a college team.

To make matters worse, Buford had not missed the state Class AAAAA semifinals, the Final Four, since 2006. By the time Buford's seniors had begun the first grade, the streak was already underway.

And then there was Buford's 35-game home-field play-off winning streak.[110]

The Buford matchup required the Bainbridge coaching staff to continue building the team's self-confidence. That meant adding to confidence in both the game preparation and the Bearcats' competitive ability. As *Psychology Today* columnist Jim Taylor, Ph.D. explained, "In reality, confidence is a skill, much like technical skills, that can be learned. Just like with any type of skill, confidence is developed through focus, effort, and repetition."[111]

So Bainbridge spent the week preparing for their underdog playoff run, not against Buford, but against "the green team".

One factor that might have made it easier to coach the confidence was the rising confidence of the coaches themselves. Privately, the Bainbridge coaches became increasingly confident in the team's growth and ability. For some that began in the practices after the hurricane, when the team's bonding elevated their performance as a team. For others, it was the blowout opening-round win over an outstanding Jones County win. Even the sportswriter from Macon had proclaimed Bainbridge's ability to "shock" teams in later rounds of the playoffs. For a few, the second-round close win against undefeated Wayne County had finally convinced them. "That's when I knew we could beat anybody," one assistant coach explained.

As *Post Searchlight* managing editor Powell Cobb believes, the Bainbridge team facing the giant that was Buford reflected the personality of its coach. "Coach Littleton is pas-

state_rankings/2020/georgia. Retrieved November 22, 2019.

110   Jeff Littleton (Bainbridge head football coach) in discussion with the author, December 3, 2019.

111   Taylor, Jim, "Sports: Introduction to Confidence," *Psychology Today*, November 9, 2009. https://www.psychologytoday.com/us/blog/the-power-prime/200911/sports-introduction-confidence. Retrieved November 22, 2019.

sionate, strong-willed and despises losing. He preaches the old Belichick 'Do your job' mantra nonstop, and drills that into his players' heads. The same goes for his coaches."[112]

For Coach Littleton, the clash with Buford was the fulfillment of promises he had made to the team five years earlier, in his first meeting with the new Bainbridge team.
"We will win, if we do things the right way. I just need you to do right. If you treat your teachers right, they will like you. If you do right, we will have success."[113]

And so it began.

Game night in Buford brought even more difficulties to the matchup, as even the weather seemed to conspire against Bainbridge. The evening was described as an "absolute frigid and rainy evening" by the NFHS broadcasting team of Brandon Joseph (color) and Chris Willingham (play-by-play). That weather surely would slow down the big-play Bainbridge offense, giving an advantage to the Buford defense.[114]

But Buford also relied on a big-play offense, scoring over 40 points in nine of its games. The youth-laden Bainbridge would have the opportunity to take the field first and establish the Bearcats as the on-the-field equal of "the green team."

Bainbridge immediately stifled the Buford offense, forcing a fourth-and-34 punt from its own end zone. That's when senior Bryce Worthy stormed through the Buford protection, blocking the punt out of the end zone. The resulting safety gave Bainbridge a quick 2-0 lead in the game's opening moments.[115]

Interestingly, even the first quarter of the game against the seemingly unbeatable Buford team, his blocked punt was

112   Powell Cobb (*Post Searchlight* managing editor) in discussion with the author, December 9, 2019.
113   "New BHS Head Football Coach Littleton Addresses the Team," YouTube video, 15:32, March 22, 2013. https://www.youtube.com/watch?v=TeDJ7G-5mX_U&feature=youtu.be. Retrieved February 20, 2019.
114   NFHS Network, "Georgia Quarterfinals: Buford vs. Bainbridge," YouTube video, 2:53:55, November 23, 2018. https://www.facebook.com/NFHSNetwork/videos/georgia-quarterfinals-buford-vs-bainbridge/2174271856154466/. Retrieved October 9, 2019.
115   Game statistics provided by the Bainbridge High School Bearcats coaching staff, and specifically by statistician Chip Ariail.

a turning point for Worthy. After the blocked punt and the next touchdown, "I knew we could win it all," he recalled.[116]

Receiving the free kick after the safety, Bainbridge immediately went into attack mode. The coaches had preached confidence all week, and the play calling let the players know that they intended to seize control of "the green team" immediately.

Sophomore quarterback Quayde Hawkins dropped back and fired a pass to senior Aaron Spivie, who caught the pass on a crossing route and sped 28 yards to the Buford 15-yard-line. The next play was a toss-sweep to Caleb McDowell, who began following his blockers to the left before abruptly cutting back to the right and outrunning the defenders to the end zone.

116   Bryce Worthy (former Bainbridge football player) in discussion with the author, December 5, 2019.

In the game's opening moments, Bainbridge had scored twice, seized control of the game, and achieved the early 9-0 lead that the broadcasters assured would "send shock waves" throughout the state.

For the Bainbridge coaches, the week of coaching confidence had paid off.

For the Bainbridge players, the week of hearing preaching that the teams were evenly matched was provably true. Faith had become sight.

For the Buford Wolves, the game had started out poorly but was about to get worse before it became any better. A fumble recovery by the Bainbridge defense gave the Bearcats a first down in the red zone.

Two Rashad Broadnax runs gave Bainbridge the ball at the Buford two-yard-line. Caleb McDowell took it from there, running straight up the middle for another touchdown and a 16-0 lead that would have been unimaginable a few weeks earlier.

While the running backs were piling up the early yards and touchdowns, another group of players made that possible. The offensive line was firing off the line of scrimmage against the opponent's defense of college players. In both of the early touchdown runs, the running back was hardly touched by a defender before scoring. That's no easy task for any offensive line, but deep into the playoffs against Buford, it's almost beyond belief.

The 16-0 lead carried Bainbridge to the half, when they led 16-13 after two Buford scores late in the half. Even then, Bainbridge blocked one of the extra points, preserving the lead by a field goal at halftime.[117]

As the teams lined up for the second-half kickoff, the wind and rain continued their assault on the teams and fans. The Bainbridge kickoff return team hit the field while the remaining players jumped up and down on the sidelines to the rhythm of the stadium music. The Buford Wolves players joined in. The excitement was building for both teams as the third quarter of the Elite Eight clash was set to begin. One of

117 Game statistics provided by the Bainbridge High School Bearcats coaching staff, and specifically by statistician Chip Ariail.

94

the teams would advance to the Final Four, the state semifinals, and a likely matchup against mighty Stockbridge.

At this level, with everything on the line, the weather was a mere nuisance as foot met leather and the ball sailed high into the frigid Atlanta sky.

The ball was caught by Caleb McDowell, who began what seemed destined to result in an unfortunate kickoff return when a Buford player broke past the protective blocking and hit McDowell at the 15-yard line. Just as the tackle began, McDowell spun his body and avoided the wrapping arms of the Buford player. The tackle never happened, and the young Bainbridge star sped right through the heart of the Buford kickoff coverage team.

Veering toward the right sideline, McDowell was now in a footrace with the lone remaining Buford defender who stood between McDowell and the end zone. The problem with the footrace for Buford was that the young dynamic Bainbridge playmakers don't lose footraces. McDowell galloped 91 yards for the kickoff return and the destination of the state's class AAAAA Final Four. Buford scored one more time to make it a three-point lead again, setting the stage for late-game drama.

Until the final minutes, the fourth quarter had remained scoreless and the Bainbridge lead remained at three points. After one missed field goal, the Buford offense marched again and had a first-and-goal with less than four minutes remaining.

If the Wolves scored a touchdown, Bainbridge would be faced with the colossal task of orchestrating a game-winning touchdown drive in the miserable weather with minimal time remaining. If Bainbridge somehow held Buford to a field goal, then the game would be tied and Bainbridge's task would be to drive to within their kicker's field goal range. Once again, the weather and scant remaining time on the clock made that highly unlikely.

An uneventful first-down run gained a couple of yards. On second down from the seven-yard-line, the entire defense saw Buford quarterback Aaron McLaughlin do what they expected, placing the ball in the hands of future Texas Longhorn Derrian Brown. After having already gained over 200 yards rushing and two touchdowns in the game, Brown was the logical choice to carry the ball and run to glory.

Then, after an artfully conducted fake, McLaughlin pulled the ball back and ran the other way toward the end zone and likely the win.

There was only one problem: Randy Fillingame.

In preseason practices, Fillingame had been moved to the inside linebacker position to get him close to the ball on almost every play. But he was still an outside linebacker at heart; he read the quarterback's fake perfectly and sprinted toward the action. Fillingame tackled the quarterback for a two-yard loss, trumping a well executed play with his quick reactive thinking and speed.[118]

Third down brought an incomplete pass, and the stage was set for a game-tying field goal attempt. Not surprisingly, Buford featured an outstanding kicker in Hayden Olsen. In the next year's Elite Eight game against Carrollton, Olsen would kick the game-winning field goal as time expired.[119]

But this year's Elite Eight kick was for the tie, and it was against a Bainbridge team that had absolutely refused to lose. The 26-yard attempt was well within his kicking range, and the distance was probably such that the wind would not affect the kick as it sailed toward the goal post.

With two minutes and eight seconds remaining in the game, the ball was snapped. The kick was up…and then it wasn't. The Bainbridge blocked field goal preserved the lead with only two minutes to go.

In most games that would have ended the suspense. This, however, was the Elite Eight of the Georgia playoffs. It was also a game involving the legendary Buford Wolves and the year's greatest underdog, the Bainbridge Bearcats.

The game's outcome wasn't anywhere close to being resolved.

After holding Bainbridge to a three-and-out, Buford

118   NFHS Network, "Georgia Quarterfinals: Buford vs. Bainbridge," YouTube video, 2:53:55, November 23, 2018. https://www.facebook.com/NFHSNetwork/videos/georgia-quarterfinals-buford-vs-bainbridge/2174271856154466/. Retrieved October 9, 2019.
119   Hart, Jeff, "'Gambler' Appling and Wolves stun No. 1 Carrollton," AccessWDUN.com, November 29, 2019. https://accesswdun.com/print/2019/11/854898/buford-vs-carrollton-quarters Retrieved December 3, 2019.

fielded the resulting punt and took possession of the ball at the Bainbridge 39-yard line. They would have yet another chance for either a game-winning touchdown or a game-tying drive.

Once again, a Bainbridge defender stepped up to make a big play at a critical time.

On second down, McLaughlin rolled to his left, looking for open receivers. Roman Harrison, the future Tennessee Volunteer, chased him down from behind and left Buford with a third-and-long. Because Buford had no timeouts remaining, the critically important sack left the Wolves with two chances at a long pass completion and no way to stop the clock. For the game, Harrison had ten tackles, five for loss, and a sack. Bryce Worthy also had ten tackles, and Randy Fillingame had eight tackles with four for lost yardage.

After two incomplete passes, the game had become an instant classic. Bainbridge had done the previously unthinkable, defeating the Buford Wolves and advancing to the Final Four.

Back home in Bainbridge, some watched the game over the internet, through the NFHS network over Facebook. Others listened over the radio. Some kept up with the results over social media, and some monitored the results by asking friends or family watching or listening.

Just about everyone in town was keeping up with the game and their heroes. Just about everyone in town knew someone associated with the team. Just about everyone in town had experienced the same or similar effects of Hurricane Michael's devastation. Just about everyone had shared the common experience of rebuilding or restoring at least some component parts of their lives after the storm.

The Bainbridge Bearcats weren't some group of spoiled athletes or prima donna personalities. They were the heroes of Bainbridge because they were overcoming great challenges just as the town was. The football team had become the Everyman of their hometown. The ascending underdogs were defeating the royalty of Georgia high school football, and they were doing it with a younger, undersized roster of players.

Some of the most fondly and vividly remembered teams in the history of American sports have been the greatest underdogs. The underdog 1969 New York Mets are possibly more revered than their fellow World Series champions, the 1986 Mets, who were much more talented overall.

Many Atlanta Braves fans remember the worst-to-first 1991 team better than any of the others in their era of great teams and elite pitching staffs. That team won the National League championship and went to extra innings of the seventh game of the World Series.

Middle-aged and older basketball fans recall the 1983 North Carolina State and 1985 Villanova national champion-ships as fondly as they do their own favorite teams.

Why?

The underdog's victory reminds us that the unlikely as-pirations in life don't have to be impossible. They remind us that the media experts and strife-stoking talk show hosts are paid to gain audiences, and not because they actually know what will happen. Epic games with unexpected results give fans the opportunity to actually become involved in the games, especially for those at the games who can elevate the crowd noise.

Underdogs remind us of the reasons that we use pro-nouns like "we" or "us" when discussing our favorite sports teams. And "we" were headed to the Final Four to compete for the state championship.

Thanks to the Bainbridge High School Bearcats, the im-possible had now become the achievable.

The State Playoffs
The Final Four (Semifinals)
Bainbridge vs. Stockbridge
November 30, 2018

From the opening quarter, this was a game like none other in the Bainbridge playoff run. Since the hurricane-week debacle against Warner Robins, Bainbridge had scored in the first quarter of every game. Against Buford, the Bearcats had rung up 16 points in the first few minutes. Landing early punches had become the calling card for Bainbridge in their post-hurricane maturity.

Not so against the 12-1 Stockbridge Tigers.

Sporting 12 seniors who would sign college football scholarships,[120] Stockbridge fielded one of the better defenses in the state of Georgia in 2018. Of all the 14 Bainbridge opponents in the regular season and playoffs, only Cairo surrendered less points. However, Stockbridge played one more playoff game while giving up only eight more points overall.

So, in the first quarter of the state semifinal game, the Bainbridge Bearcats were held scoreless. That might not be too surprising, since playing in the Final Four was a new thing for the current students at Bainbridge High School. In fact, their last Final Four team included an all-star safety named Kirby Smart. The 2018 season marked the silver anniversary of that 1993 team. Over those 25 years, as Coach Smart was racking up more national championship and conference championship rings than he can probably even remember, Bainbridge had been striving to once again play on the big stage. Coach Littleton and his staff had built Bainbridge into a winning program, and they now had the opportunity to take the next step.

And there they were. Unfortunately, the scoreboard displayed a zero after the first quarter. Then, the same result repeated itself for the second period and Bainbridge trailed at halftime.

Thankfully, football games are not decided solely by offense. The Bainbridge defense also held Stockbridge scoreless in the first quarter. Even after the Tigers' lone score late in the second quarter, Bainbridge blocked the extra point to leave the game at 6-0 going into intermission.

Aaron Spivey, who had blocked a punt for a safety the previous week against Buford, blocked the extra point to maintain some of the momentum for Bainbridge going into the second half.[121]

The third quarter, fittingly, was also scoreless. Despite the numbers on the scoreboard, the Bainbridge offense was

120   Stockbridge High School, "Signing Day 2019," February 26, 2019. https://schoolwires.henry.k12.ga.us/Page/122892. Retrieved November 26, 2019.
121   Game statistics provided by the Bainbridge High School Bearcats coaching staff, and specifically by statistician Chip Ariail.

actually moving the ball but was unable to convert yardage into points. In the first three quarters, they mounted drives of 13, 11, and 8 plays that produced no points, with two of the three drives ending in turnovers. While the turnovers were discouraging, the ability to move the ball against Stockbridge left the coaches, players, and fans with good reason for optimism as the fourth quarter began.

Then, as the final period began, the circumstances became much worse with a Stockbridge score to make the lead 13-0. For a team whose offense could move the ball but not the scoreboard, two scores looked like a high hurdle to clear in the span of just one quarter. The ability of the Stockbridge offense to consume clock time made it even more difficult.

On the ensuing kickoff, Coach Littleton and his staff were determined to be the aggressors. A trick-play lateral on the kickoff return by Aaron Spivey advanced to the 40-yard line but was called back because of a penalty. Even with the penalty, the message was sent to the players that they were executing their game plan aggressively to overcome the deficit and capture the game.

A critical third-down catch by freshman Deyon "Smoke" Bouie saved the drive and advanced Bainbridge beyond the shadow of its own goal line. When asked if that third-down pass was one of the year's most important plays, offensive coordinator Mike Harville agreed. "That play kind of got lost with all the other miraculous plays," he said with a laugh. "That play really set up the rest of the fourth quarter for us."[122] Then sophomore quarterback, Quayde Hawkins, completed three straight passes and then scrambled for a first down across midfield.

Then, lightning struck. Actually it was smoke, as Deyon "Smoke" Bouie took a quick pass at the line of scrimmage, crossed the entire field and weaved through defenders for a critical 39-yard gain and a first-and-goal. A quick pass from Hawkins to McDowell resulted in a touchdown and capped an 11-play, 95-yard drive.[123]

122   Mike Harville (Bainbridge offensive football coach) in discussion with the author, December 14, 2019.
123   Bainbridge Bearcats vs. Stockbridge Tigers, YouTube video, 2:35:38, November 30, 2018. https://www.youtube.com/watch?v=6EcQuli5GXE. Re-

The score was now 13-7, and Bainbridge was back in the game. The Cinderella story that was the Bearcats seemed to possibly have another miracle chapter, but only if their defense could stop the clock-eating Stockbridge offense.

After two plays, they faced a third-and-long but had already gotten the clock down to 5:42 remaining.

Stockbridge called the most critical time out in the game to make their decision from among several choices. One choice was to run the ball, let the clock wind down to around five minutes remaining, punt the ball, and let their defense hold Bainbridge on its final drive. Another choice was to throw a safe pass, meaning a short screen pass or pass to a wide receiver at the line of scrimmage, and hope to get a first down but still run down the clock if unsuccessful.

The third option was to run a pass play, letting the quarterback find an open receiver or scramble for the first down if nothing was open. This option was appealing because it was aggressive.

So, after deliberating during their timeout, the Stockbridge coaching staff chose...wait for it...none of the above.

The ball was snapped to the Stockbridge quarterback, who threw a backward pass to a wide receiver. Because it was a backward pass, it was considered a lateral, so the receiver could either run with the ball or throw a pass himself.

Looking deep to the opposite sideline, the Stockbridge receiver launched a pass to another receiver who was streaking down the sideline with a Bainbridge cornerback in hot pursuit.

On this monumental play in the game, the newfound maturity of the Bainbridge players after Hurricane Michael came into play.

The beauty of this trick play is that, although it's risky, it takes advantage of the fact that most safeties on opposing defenses will sprint up toward the wide receiver who caught the backward-lateral pass. So when the receiver throws the pass downfield, there is usually no safety back there to help with the deep-field pass coverage.

The Stockbridge coaches knew that Bainbridge had a

The banner said it all: SMALL TOWN BIG DREAMS. In a way, the town became even smaller after Hurricane Michael devastated the city of Bainbridge because it brought the town's people closer together. The football team's second chance against Warner Robins became a metaphor for the entire town's comeback after the damage caused by Hurricane Michael.

freshman, Zion Bouie, in deep coverage, and that freshmen typically fall for such trick-plays.

While they were officially still ninth-graders, the Bainbridge rookie players were no longer freshmen. At least not in experience, after a full season, the hurricane, and the run deep into the playoffs against Wayne County, Buford, and now Stockbridge.

Although the ball was thrown well, before the receiver could make the catch, safety Zion Bouie flashed in front of the pass and intercepted the ball at the 40-yard line. Sprinting down the sideline, he dove for the end zone ahead of a would-be tackler, landing safely beyond the goal line. The result was a pick-six touchdown and an amazing 14 points in just 69 seconds of time on the game clock.[124]

The secret to Zion Bouie's big play on the big stage was the fact that he was on the field at all. "He was only a freshman, but he forced himself into the lineup by his hard work and dedication," explained Coach Littleton. "He was already an outstanding athlete, but he forced us to play him because he worked so hard and improved so much so quickly."[125]

A few seconds before, the coaches, players, and fans of Stockbridge might have thought their lead was insurmountable.

If so, they didn't know Bainbridge.

A few moments before, Zion Bouie's cousin, Deyon, had made the difference on the offensive scoring drive. The future clearly looked bright for Bainbridge with young players like the Bouie cousins, quarterback Quayde Hawkins, and of course Caleb McDowell.

Then, if the game could not have become any more suspenseful, Stockbridge responded immediately with a 31-yard pass down the same sideline where the interception had happened moments earlier. This 12-1 team was ready to strike a fatal blow to the Bainbridge state championship dreams.

The clock wound down as the Stockbridge drive progressed. With under two minutes remaining, a pass lofted to-

124 Id.
125 Jeff Littleton (Bainbridge head football coach) in discussion with the author, December 3, 2019.

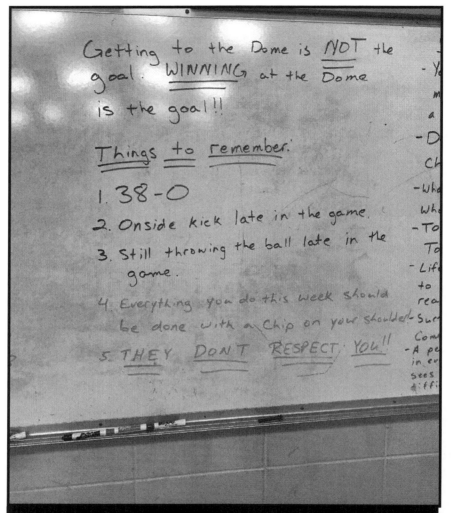

Getting to the Dome is _NOT_ the
goal. _WINNING_ at the Dome
is the goal!!

Things to remember:

1. 38-0
2. Onside kick late in the game.
3. Still throwing the ball late in the game.
4. Everything you do this week should be done with a chip on your shoulder.
5. _THEY DON'T RESPECT YOU!!_

During the week of the state championship game, the dry-erase board in the Bainbridge locker room said it all. The onside kick and late-game passing by Warner Robins weren't exactly forgotten by the Bainbridge coaches and players.

Throughout game week, the board reminded the players of both the challenges that lay ahead and the remarkable journey they have already traveled as a team. The scene was set for a championship rematch for the ages. (Photo courtesy of team chaplain, Rev. Steve Brooks).

ward the front corner of the end zone found its Yashn McKee, who stretched the football over the pylon. The result was a touchdown, and Stockbridge had captured the late lead at 19-14 with 1:52 remaining in the game.

The future looked bleak.

At least it would for most teams.

Once again, Bainbridge would have the opportunity to pull off another improbable miracle, but this time it appeared that their worst enemy was the game clock that only had 112 seconds remaining.

Then came the kickoff.

Stockbridge launched a squib kick, meaning that they kicked it hard on the ground toward the players in the middle of the field rather than the speedy kick returners. Things didn't start off well with the kickoff return, as someone in the crowd fumbled or bobbled the ball and it went to the ground.

To make matters worse, the ball was picked up by a line-backer rather than a speedster from the offense.

That's when the fun began.

The linebacker happened to be Randy Fillingame, de-scribed by coaches as a coach on the field because of his un-derstanding of the game. Fillingame ran briefly with the ball, and then, while being tackled, lateraled the ball to the team's most dynamic offensive player, Caleb McDowell.

In a moment that will live in the history of Bainbridge football, and even the city's history, McDowell zipped through the kickoff coverage team with his elite speed and sprinted down the same sideline route that his teammate Zion Bouie had taken just moments before on his pick-six touchdown.

Once again, for the second time in less than four min-utes, Stockbridge saw Bainbridge seize the lead from them. For the second time in less than four minutes, their hearts were figuratively broken.

After scoring no points through three-and-a-half quar-ters, Bainbridge torched Stockbridge for 20 points within five minutes.

Bainbridge had pulled off another miracle ending, but there was just one problem. When McDowell scored the go-ahead touchdown on the kickoff return, the clock still read 1:37

remaining.

After a squib kick with no return, the Stockbridge offense began their drive. After some completed passes and first downs, Bainbridge held firm and forced a fourth-and-ten conversion attempt near the red zone. Stockbridge quarterback Jevon McDonald dropped back, surveyed the receivers and threw a rifle-pass to a receiver at the first-down marker.

Enter Bryce Worthy.

Less than a yard shy of the first-down marker, Bainbridge senior Bryce Worthy laid a hit on the receiver that put him down and preserved the victory. On the stat sheet it was just another tackle for a player who had made plenty of them. For the team, however, the hit he laid on the Stockbridge receiver extinguished all of the Tigers' dreams to play in the state championship game.

The game, the suspense, and the twenty-five-year drought of state championship games were all mercifully over.

Bainbridge was going to compete in the state championship game in Mercedes-Benz Stadium in Atlanta. And they would face the team that had embarrassed them in the wake of the hurricane, the Warner Robins Demons.

Bainbridge would bring the same players, coaches, uniforms, and equipment to the championship game, but they would not bring the same team. Too much had happened. Too much had been endured. Too much had been overcome. The result was of course uncertain, but Warner Robins would face a different opponent this time.

But would it be enough?

Chapter 7

The Championship

"The fun is in the winning."
- Coach Gene Stallings

The State Playoffs
The state championship game
Bainbridge vs. Warner Robins
December 11, 2018

All across the world, children and teenagers dream of starring in championship games on the big stage. Kids playing stickball in the streets of New York imitate the batting stances of Yankees and Mets sluggers. On the frozen tundra of ballfields in Wisconsin, youngsters toss footballs, aspiring to become the next Aaron Rodgers or Brett Favre of the Green Bay Packers. In college towns, kids grow up hoping to one day win their team's rivalry game and become the darling of local fans, media, and of course the girls. In Minnesota's arctic winters, young hockey players dream of winning the Stanley Cup or beating the Russians in the Olympics. In the gyms of Los Angeles, fans of Lebron James or Anthony Davis dream of one day taking their place on the Lakers. They also wonder if Magic or Kareem could really have been as great as their dads claim.

Many if not most of those dreams have two things in common: winning the biggest games and the biggest arenas.

The grandest arena in America is, in the minds of many, the Mercedes-Benz stadium in Atlanta. Almost everything about the stadium is state-of-the-art and often beyond the imagination of most sports fans. It's somehow both an outdoor and an indoor stadium, described as an outdoor stadium with a roof. The video board is a colossal 62,350 square feet. The

108

price tag totaled an equally imposing amount of $1.6 billion. If you are watching games from a seat at a bar, the stadium sports a 100-yard long bar parallel to the football field.[126]

And speaking of football, the stadium was built for both types of football. Entire sections of seating are retractable, allowing the stadium to quickly convert to a more cozy seating total of 42,500 for soccer matches.[127]

The Mercedes-Benz stadium was unveiled, just over a year earlier, as the premier sports venue in the world. Even before it opened, it had landed two of the most prestigious events in all of American sports. In January of 2018, the stadium had hosted college football's national championship game, and luckily enough, it featured the home state's Georgia Bulldogs. To make the story even better, the second-year Georgia coach was none other than Bainbridge's favorite son, Kirby Smart. Smart led his team to complete domination of their opponent, the Alabama Crimson Tide in the first half, and came up just short in an overtime thriller in the debut of quarterback Tua Tagovailoa on the national stage.

A few weeks after the Bainbridge playoff run, in February of 2019, the Super Bowl was played in the still-new stadium, as a worldwide audience watched the New England Patriots continue their dynastic rule of the National Football League with a win over the Los Angeles Rams.

So the most luxurious stadium in the world had also become one of its biggest stages. On this stage, the state championship games of Georgia High School would be played. The elite teams of each classification, performing at the highest levels, would compete for their place in the rich history of Georgia football. Classic games and legendary performances were possible in each time.

In the 2018 state championship games, one game appeared to stand as an exception. In the AAAAA matchup between Warner Robins and Bainbridge, the question of which was the better team seemed to have already been decided. Calling it a convincing win would be a charitable description.

126   https://mercedesbenzstadium.com/the-stadium/. Retrieved November 22, 2019.
127   Id.

109

The 38-0 blowout was more like a demolition.

At least that's what the outside world saw. In the Bainbridge locker room, they fully understood that the team demolished on that late October night in Warner Robins was not the same team that would face them for the rematch. Maturity, togetherness, and experience were weapons added to the Bainbridge arsenal over the last six weeks.

The rematch factor

And then there's the dynamic of the rematch. For some reason, football teams often have enjoyed great success in a rematch of an earlier loss. In December of 2017, the Georgia Bulldogs won the SEC title by besting the Auburn team that had won their first game at Auburn. In 1996, the University of Florida won the national championship by defeating the Florida State team that had beaten them a few weeks earlier.

In 2011, Alabama pitched a 21-0 shutout of the LSU team that had edged them in overtime in the Game of the Century. Almost 60 years ago, LSU lost another rematch by the same 21-0 score. After defeating Ole Miss 7-3 in the regular season, the Sugar Bowl featured the rematch of these two top-five teams, with the #2-ranked Ole Miss team shutting out the #3-ranked Tigers.

Ohio State's legendary coach Woody Hayes predicted that, after his team defeated UCLA, his Buckeyes would see them again. Sure enough, the Rose Bowl featured the UCLA Bruins upsetting the #1-ranked Ohio State team and costing them a national championship.

Whatever the reasons, and they probably vary between rematches, the result of the rematch is typically not a done deal in the sport of football.

Despite the first game's result, there were some interesting angles for the media.

Some of the best news, however, was not news at

(Above and below) Fans and cheerleaders gave the Bainbridge team an unforgettable sendoff, showing the support, appreciation, and love from a home-town to its team.

all, at least not publicly. One of the quiet messages from the coaching staff during the entire week was respect, or more specifically disrespect. Late in the teams' first meeting, Warner Robins executed an onside kick to regain the ball after a touchdown and keep running up the score against the hurricane-affected Bainbridge team. Late in the game, with the result long-settled, the coaches were still calling passing plays to inflate the final margin of victory.

Many words could be used to describe the Warner Robins victory that night, including powerful, effective, and overwhelming. As for words like "class" and "sportsmanship," maybe not so much.

If that didn't say enough about the Warner Robins program, the breaking news during championship week confirmed everything that the Bainbridge players, coaches, and fans had seen in October. In the height of pridefulness, during game week, word leaked out that Warner Robins had already ordered their state championship rings.

On the dry-erase board in the Bainbridge locker room, a hand-written message from the coaches, written by Coach Kineard, set the tone for their preparation:

Things to remember
38-0
Onside kick late in the game
Still throwing the ball late in the game
Everything you do this week should be done with a chip on your shoulder
THEY DON'T RESPECT YOU!![128]

If this were a movie, the Warner Robins team might be dismissed as too predictable of a villain, running up the score after the hurricane and ordering the championship rings before the game. As the great American writer Mark Twain once penned, "Truth is stranger than fiction, but it is because fiction is obliged to stick to possibilities; Truth isn't."

The coaches didn't preach revenge, but rather a tight focus on each person's responsibilities for the game.

---

128   Rev. Steve Brooks (Bainbridge team chaplain) in discussion with the author, December 3, 2019.

The conduct of the opponents wasn't the only news that was closely held in the Bainbridge locker room.

The coaches spent the week implementing their game plan on each side of the ball. Coach Jeff Littleton had decided to keep his offensive game plan in place for the rematch, even though the first game resulted in a shutout loss. "The first game was so unusual, with missed practices and distractions, that the game plan was not executed in the way it could have been, and that was understandable," Littleton explained. "Our goal was to get the ball into the hands of our playmakers and put them into a position to succeed. We expected to make some big plays against Warner Robins, and we used a game plan to make that happen."

While the offensive game plan remained similar, championship game week saw many more changes made on the defensive side of the ball. "We already knew that Warner Robins had a dynamic offense," explained co-defensive coordinator Brian Hill. "We worked to disguise coverages to force their quarterback into some early mistakes. We expected them to make adjustments during the game, but we especially wanted to get to him early."

That quarterback happened to be named Dylan Fromm, who was named 2018 Mr. Georgia as the outstanding senior player in the state. Fromm passed for over 4,100 yards and 44 touchdowns as a senior, and was named the Class AAAAA player of the year. There were actually two reasons why the Bainbridge coaches understood that Warner Robins would make adjustments during the game. One was the elite coaching staff led by head coach Mike Chastain, and the other was that Fromm himself was a 4.0, straight-A student who finished in the top five of his class academically. Dylan Fromm ultimately signed to play football at Mercer University.

Dylan wasn't the only Fromm posing a challenge for Bainbridge. His brother, Tyler, was a 6-foot-4 tight end with elite skills who signed to play football at Auburn University.

The Fromm name stands tall in the world of Georgia high school football, as their older brother, Jake Fromm, was a star at Warner Robins and became the University of Georgia's quarterback as a freshman. Big brother Jake won the

SEC championship his freshman year and gave an outstanding performance in the national championship game. He led the Bulldogs to the SEC East division championship three years in a row.

So for fans of the Georgia Bulldogs, the rematch created a clash between the alma mater of their head coach (Kirby Smart) and the team of their quarterback (Jake Fromm).

Thankfully, circumstances intervened and gave the coaches, especially the defensive coaches, some extra days to prepare. The Atlanta United professional soccer team had made the playoffs and had a home game scheduled for the weekend on which the games were originally scheduled. Accordingly, the state championship games were rescheduled and the Class AAAAA title game was now set for December 11.

Interestingly, that brought another good benefit for the Bainbridge team. Along with additional time to prepare, the December 11 date marked the 36th anniversary of the school's other state championship, won on December 11, 1982.

One of the great traditions of football has always been the mascots and banners on the field as the crowd anticipates the teams running into the arena. The University of Colorado runs a live buffalo across the field to the delight of their fans. The Ohio State University band stands in a formation creating the word "OHIO," and a different person at each game is bestowed with the honor of "dotting the i." In the 1980s, when "The U" became a fixture in sports, the University of Miami famously created fog in the tunnels for their players to dramatically run through onto the field.

In the Bainbridge vs. Warner Robins championship game, both schools created an energetic and lively atmosphere for their players and fans for the dramatic entrance. For Bainbridge, however, one banner told the story of their entire season and journey together.

Rather than enlarged photos or graphics, or even rhyming lyrics, the banner sported a simple but profound and powerful message.

SMALL TOWN
BIG DREAMS

That one message, just four words, described the entire turnaround of the Bainbridge Bearcats. It also explained why thousands of fans had traveled all the way to Atlanta during the middle of a week to cheer on their team.

The banner did not merely name the high school, the mascot, the players, the coaches, or even the game of football. The message was about the entire town. This was THEIR team. The people of Bainbridge, and the football players and coaches, had survived and endured Hurricane Michael together. They had grieved medical trauma together. In the wake of the storm, they had fed each other, clothed each other, delivered water to each other, housed each other, counseled with each other, wept on each other's shoulders, covered each other's roofs, and shared their remaining worldly possessions with each other.

In the depths of recovery and a quest for normalcy, the Bainbridge Bearcats had become a point of focus. In each game of the playoffs, the fans returned the favor. "This team was so important to our community," explained the team chaplain, Reverend Steve Brooks." The team became the rallying point and great conversation while people were still suffering. And the people of Bainbridge were there for them. I've been going to the state championship games in Atlanta with my family for 25 years. I can't ever remember a louder and maybe even a larger crowd supporting just one team. The fans were part of the team through the entire playoff run."[129]

The championship game cheering didn't begin at the stadium. Before leaving for Atlanta, the team buses took a victory tour by the elementary and middle schools, giving the young kids a chance to cheer on their sports heroes, many of whom were their older siblings, cousins, or neighbors. "That was really special," one of the coaches explained. "It meant a lot to the players and to the kids at the other schools. That was a meaningful moment for everyone."

Back in the locker room, the team went through its final preparations before the game began. The team chaplain, Rev. Steve Brooks, addressed the team for the customary ten minutes. The scripture was from the Bible's book of Romans, chapter 12, verses 9-13. The devotion focused on everything that the team had endured and overcome together. "The scripture speaks of loving one another with a brotherly love and being devoted to one another," Brooks recalled. "We challenged the team to play for the man next to him. We had been through so much but we went through it together."

Then, Coach Littleton gave the pregame remarks to the team. He spoke of their togetherness, and their trust in each other. He reminded them to do their jobs on each play and their brothers on the team would do the same. He talked about remaining focused, and standing firm in the quest to finish the game as strongly as they begin it.

Then, he spoke of savoring the moment of the big game and their closeness as a team. In fact, much of the week was spent trying to help the players achieve a balance of preparing thoroughly but still enjoying the week of the game. It wasn't enough to just get to the game in Atlanta, but that didn't mean they couldn't enjoy the experience of game week.

"I've been a part of underdog teams and part of teams that were supposed to win," Coach Littleton said. "Sometimes, when you're supposed to win, the pressure is so great

---

129   Rev. Steve Brooks (Bainbridge team chaplain) in discussion with the author, December 3, 2019.

that game week can be miserable. We as coaches didn't want our players to go through that, so we've worked hard to make sure they stayed focused but still treasure the experience. No one ever knows whether they will have an opportunity like this again."[130]

So with the thousands of cheering fans in the seats, and with the cheerleaders, mascot, banner and others on the field, the Bainbridge team crawled like bearcats onto the playing field of America's grandest sports stage ripping through the banner's words "Small Town Big Dreams."

It was not, however, their first moment on the field. The coaches had made sure the players had abundant, if not slightly excessive time in their pregame walk-through to absorb the atmosphere and the images of the immense stadium. The goal was to give the players enough time to become familiar with standing in there, so when they took the field, the focus would remain there. The team also watched one of the earlier championship games together, giving them even more time to develop comfort with their surroundings.

But now, it was game time. Now it was time to perform.

The game started slowly. For most of the first quarter, the team swapped three-and-outs. In fact, the first seven drives of the game resulted in punts.

Then, with about three minutes remaining in the first period of play, Warner Robins attempted a punt that Bainbridge blocked at the line of scrimmage. Anthony Brooks fielded the blocked punt and sprinted untouched to the end zone for the first score of the championship game.

From time to time, all football teams may occasionally block a kick or return a kick for a touchdown. However, from year to year, it seems like the same teams end up blocking many more kicks or enjoying big kick returns than others. In college, the Virginia Tech Hokies have long been known for blocking more kicks and making more special teams plays than other programs. Other schools might seem to excel in kick returns. Usually, the schools that excel in special teams find themselves ranked high in the polls. So how do teams remain consistently

130   Jeff Littleton (Bainbridge head football coach) in discussion with the author, December 3, 2019.

good in blocking or returning kicks when players come and go?

In one word, the answer is: coaching.

Against mighty Buford, Bainbridge blocked two kicks. Against Stockbridge in the Final Four, Bainbridge blocked a kick. For the year, the Bearcats blocked an imposing nine kicks (two punts and seven field goals or extra points), meaning that the special teams are a priority in the Bainbridge program. "You win with defense and special teams, and that's why we spend so much time on that part of the game," explained Coach Littleton.[131]

So the hard work and preparation on special teams paid off immediately for Bainbridge. So, too, did the defensive adjustments of disguising coverages. The Bearcats had forced punts on the Demons' first four possessions. On its next possession after the blocked punt, Warner Robins came out throwing, determined to have a possession without a punt.

And that's exactly what they got.

The Demons' possession ended with a touchdown, but not quite the way they had planned. Quarterback Dylan Fromm read the coverages, dropped back, and fired a pass toward a receiver on their right sideline. The disguised coverages worked again, and Bryce Worthy intercepted the pass at the 32-yard line and raced into the end zone for a pick-six touchdown.[132]

Bainbridge had scored 14 points in just 14 seconds of playing time.

The next Warner Robins drive was only three plays, and this time it ended not with a punt, but with a lost fumble by Warner Robins at their own 24-yard line. Inside linebacker Randy Fillingame had blitzed on the play and found himself in the backfield with the chance to recover the fumble, which is exactly what he did. Now, with the ball and a two-touchdown lead, Bainbridge tossed the ball to their dynamic playmaker, Caleb McDowell.

No surprise there.

---

131   Id.
132   Game statistics provided by the Bainbridge High School Bearcats coaching staff, and specifically by statistician Chip Ariail.

But what came next was a surprise. Rather than running down their right sideline, McDowell stopped and threw a 24-yard pass to teammate Aaron Spivie despite the fact that Spivie was covered by two Warner Robins defenders. McDowell didn't just throw it up for grabs; he lofted the ball to where only one of the defenders had a marginal chance at the ball and his receiver didn't have to fight for it. It was a perfectly thrown pass. "This is a play that we pretty much worked on all year, and you just have to have the right situation to run it," Littleton explained.

At the end of the first quarter, Bainbridge had stormed to a 21-0 lead.

And the assault wasn't over.

In the opening moments of the second quarter, quarterback Quayde Hawkins faked a handoff to a running back and fired a dead-on pass to Aaron Spivie, who was running a quick slant route toward the middle from the right side. Spivie, who had made a leaping touchdown catch a few minutes earlier, caught the pass and dashed toward the middle of the field. Only a Demons defensive back with a good angle managed to tackle him after a 48-yard gain. Two plays later, Caleb McDowell ran for a 9-yard touchdown. After the extra point, Bainbridge held a 28-0 lead.[133]

After a Warner Robins score mid-way through the second quarter, the halftime break brought a score of 28-7 and plenty of delighted Bearcats fans.

One of the people who wasn't quite ready to be delighted, however, was Coach Littleton. For him, this was familiar ground. "I've played and coached in state championship games where we won, and when we've lost, and the only difference in the two was whether we executed for the entire length of the game. That's what determines if you win or if you lose."

The Bainbridge coaches spent halftime preparing their players to stand firm when Warner Robins struck back. "We knew they would have a run in the second half," recalled Coach Brian Hill. "We had a team of winners, but we knew they did too. They were too talented not to make a good run at this thing in the second half."

133   Id.

Focused and finishing…the two words from the pre-game remarks once again took center stage at halftime. Littleton stood on top of a table, speaking forcefully to the team and reminding them that they still had two quarters left to play.

As it turned out, the team had much more than two quarters left to play.

The second half began much as the first, with Bainbridge scoring first. This time, it was cornerback Deyon Bouie who picked off a Fromm pass and sped 30 yards for the pick-six touchdown. For Deyon, the moment was a metaphor for how his hard work had propelled him to his role as a leading defender for the Bearcats. In August, he was competing for the quarterback position. Now, on the big stage, he scored what would become a critically important touchdown. Coach Randy Hill, who coached high school All-American (and future college and pro player) Greg Reid at Lowndes County High School, compared Deyon Bouie to his former star pupil. "He reminds me a lot of Greg at that age, with the explosive speed and the desire to work hard and practice hard."[134]

Deyon's cousin, Zion Bouie, also played an outstanding game in the championship. Like his cousin, Zion began the year as an unknown freshman who just outworked other players and improved. Like his cousin, Zion stepped up in a big way on the big stage. "Zion made a number of open-field tackles that were a big part of our winning the championship game," Littleton recalled.[135] After the pick-six, the score stood at 35-7 in the second half. The odds of a Bainbridge victory were improving with every second ticking off the game clock.

If the second half were described with a movie title, it would probably have been *The Empire Strikes Back*. Unfortunately, Deyon Bouie's pick-six with 9:42 left in the third quarter was the last Bainbridge score of the second half. The rest of the scoring, and there was plenty, belonged to Warner Robins.

Demons quarterback Dylan Fromm passed for an impressive 274 yards and two touchdowns, doing much of his damage in the second half. Trailing 35-21 with eight minutes

134   Randy Hill (Bainbridge defensive football coach) in discussion with the author, November 22, 2019.
135   Jeff Littleton (Bainbridge head football coach) in discussion with the author, December 3, 2019.

remaining in the game, Dylan threw a backward lateral pass to his brother, future Auburn tight end Tyler Fromm. After running a couple of steps, Tyler stopped and threw a pass back to his brother Dylan, who weaved through defenders for the third Demons touchdown of the second half. The once-massive lead had been carved down to a difference of one touchdown.

Finally, with 1:16 left in the fourth quarter, Warner Robins scored a touchdown on another Dylan Fromm touchdown pass to even the score. All of the big plays, the huge lead, and everything else done by Bainbridge had now been matched by their opponent. "Some things didn't work out in the fourth quarter," Littleton said, "but we kept our composure, we kept fighting, and we waited for our chance."

But Warner Robins had just scored on three of their last four possessions, and they weren't finished. On the final drive of the game, the Demons marched to the Bainbridge red zone once again. On fourth down, Warner Robins lined up to kick a field goal with only six seconds to go. The game, the season, the championship, the big dreams of a small town, and the game of a lifetime stood in grave jeopardy.

The odds are heavily against any individual kick being blocked, but then this was a kick with the opponent wearing uniforms sporting the name Bainbridge. The earlier blocked kick, the blocked kicks in the playoffs, and the seemingly endless special teams practice time were the source of both hope and preparation.

"It was nerve racking," recalled Littleton in a massive understatement, "but we had confidence in our special teams and our ability to block kicks. We had to trust them. We hadn't shown pressure up the middle all year, so Warner Robins hadn't seen that, and then Roman Harrison just really made a good play up the middle."

"I just hoped that someone wanted it so badly that they would make it happen," recalled Coach Brian Hill.

"I didn't know if they would block it, but I knew they could," said Coach Randy Hill. "They were prepared for that situation."

But the best description came from Coach Dollar. "I told Roman Harrison to go block that kick," he recalled. That's be-

cause great players make great plays. That's what they do."[136]

As the holder waited for the ball to be snapped by the center, the scoreboard read third-and-3 from the ten yard line. The clock read 0:06. The ball was snapped, the holder did his job perfectly, the kicker smacked the ball, and the television camera followed the trajectory of the ball toward the goal post.

But then, the camera jerked back toward the players, because there was no ball sailing toward the goal post after all.

Senior defensive lineman Roman Harrison, the future Tennessee Volunteer and defensive leader of the team, had blocked the field goal. The game was not lost, at least not during four quarters. The Bainbridge fans screamed wildly. The momentum, owned by Warner Robins during their four touchdowns, had been seized once again by Bainbridge.

An absolutely crazy game had now crossed the line into insanity.

During the first overtime, each team kicked a field goal,

136   Joe Dollar (Bainbridge defensive football coach) in discussion with the author, December 16, 2019.

so the game progressed into a second overtime. Once again, each team kicked a field goal during their possession. The state championship headed into a third overtime period.

On the third play of the third overtime, the Bainbridge quarterback placed the ball into the running back's arms heading to the left side, but actually he didn't. "It was a read-option play," explained offensive coordinator Joe Harville. "That means the quarterback reads whether the defenders went for the running back, and if so, he has the option to keep the ball."[137] Executing a historically good fake hand-off, he pulled the ball back from the running back and sprinted to the right. While most of the Demons defense attacked the running back whom they thought was carrying the ball, Hawkins ran the other way. One defensive back made it to Hawkins, but the sophomore quarterback, who had to fight for the starting position in August, scored the go-ahead touchdown in triple overtime.

Once again, Warner Robins had the ball. Once again, they placed their hopes in the arm of Dylan Fromm. Once again, the Bainbridge defense had to step up.

Once again, Deyon "Smoke" Bouie did exactly that.

On fourth down, with the game on the line, Fromm threw a pass to a receiver streaking down the right sideline on a go-route. It was scarily similar to the routes that his older brother Jake has thrown so well at the University of Georgia. Like his brother, he artfully placed the ball near the outside shoulder of the receiver so no one else would be able to make the play if he couldn't.

Despite the excellent pass, Bainbridge cornerback Deyon Bouie blanketed the receiver with excellent coverage and there was just no way that the pass could be completed.

The ball fell harmlessly to the ground.

Bainbridge players, coaches, cheerleaders, and anyone else who could manage it stormed the field. Coaches and teammates congratulated each other. Many from both teams congratulated each other too, on the magnificent game that had just concluded.

Fans posted selfies from the game on social media.

---

137   Joe Harville (Bainbridge offensive football coach) in discussion with the author, December 14, 2019.

One videoed the final play and posted a profane but joyous reaction on YouTube. People from Bainbridge were texting and e-mailing and Instant Messaging congratulations from just about everywhere. The Georgia Bulldogs' Coach Kirby Smart texted Coach Littleton immediately to congratulate him and let him know that he had been more than a little worried in the fourth quarter.

Many would say that the team's season had ended, but really it was an entire city's journey that had resulted in victory for them all.

The banner had it right: small town big dreams.

Indeed.

Chapter 8

Small Town
Big Dreams

"God gave us the gift of life;
it is up to us
to give ourselves
the gift of living well."
- Volatire

The field that had once featured two ferociously competing teams now only held one. That team included the coaches, players, cheerleaders, and thousands of fans from Bainbridge. The Mercedes-Benz stadium, known as one of the world's great stages for sporting events, now included an actual stage on the field. No, there wasn't a concert scheduled, but instead a championship team that had just completed a three overtime concerto of determination, perseverance, and intensity.

Players held up the early newspaper editions proclaiming them as the champions that they had now become. Coaches and players alike hoisted the state championship trophy to the delighted crowd.

It had been a game for the ages. Theo Dorsey, the host of WALB News 10's television show *Sports Talk with Theo Dorsey*, called the game "the wildest, roller coaster ride to a state championship that I've witnessed."[138]

Afterward, the triumphant crowd and its heroes returned home. Two months and one day after the hurricane had hit, there was still plenty of hard work ahead for many if not most in the community. Many homes were still uninhabitable, and plenty of others partially so. New clothes were gradually purchased to replace lost wardrobes.

Depending on the extent of the damage to their homes, families had differing timetables for their returns to normalcy. For

---

138   WALB, *"Sports Talk* with Theo Dorsey" YouTube Video, 20:23, December 19, 2018. https://www.youtube.com/watch?v=Mxx0ZHyMJzU. Retrieved October 9, 2019.

the community a new normal had emerged. Now, the people down the street became the people who had helped cover your roof, or whom you had given rides to when they couldn't get to work or school. The new normal meant communities in which people knew each other better because of their common experiences together.

There was also a new normal at Bainbridge High School. A championship ring was not something earned once upon a time in 1982; it was a real and present event. Another real and present event was the respect that the coaches had spent the entire year challenging players to earn. Hoisting the trophy was one sign of inescapably earning the respect of the world of Georgia sports. Jeff Littleton was named the Class AAAAA Coach of the Year. Senior defensive lineman Roman Harrison, who seized victory from the jaws of defeat with his historic blocked field goal, was named the Class AAAAA Defensive Player of the Year and first-team All-State by the *Atlanta Journal-Constitution*. Linebacker Randy Fillingame, who unselfishly moved to inside linebacker at the coaches' request, was named first-team All-State as well.

Fillingame and fellow linebacker Bryce Worthy signed football scholarships, taking their talents to LaGrange College. To no one's surprise, both players made an immediate impact for the Panthers in the 2019 season, combining for over 100 tackles and three sacks.

Harrison signed with the University of Tennessee, where he gradually emerged as the freshman contributor fans expected. He registered his first collegiate sack in the Volunteers victory over UAB.

Littleton, asked more times than he could remember what this championship meant, said the most important thing was what this meant to the kids. On the one hand, it might seem like the impact is lessened for someone like Littleton, who has won state championships as a head coach, an assistant, and as a player. Between Littleton, his brother-in-law Brian Hill, and his father-in-law Randy Hill, they have a whopping 12 state championship rings. Now that's a family of winners.

But despite the past successes, this championship was different. "I've never seen a team go through as much as these guys and respond with such discipline and courage," he added.

Coach Latavius Davis agreed about discipline and courage. "Coach Littleton did an outstanding job of molding these young men into champions, even with the hurricane and other tragedies."[139]

In the American tradition of great champions and championships, the city of Bainbridge held a victory parade. The event was absolutely held for the team and coaches, but in a way, it was also for the city itself.

Teams at all levels represent their cities, especially during difficult times. Many remember the first New Orleans Saints game in the Super Dome after Hurricane Katrina, and the crowd's deafening roar when the Saints blocked an Atlanta Falcons punt in the first quarter for a scoop-and-score. After Hurricane Andrew assaulted the southern tip of Florida in 1992, the University of Miami Hurricanes made it all the way to the national championship game and featured the Heisman Trophy winner. In 2011, after one of American history's worst tornado outbreaks destroyed much of Tuscaloosa, the University of Alabama won the national championship. In the 1986-87 college basketball season, the Providence College Friars

---

139   Latavius Davis (Bainbridge defensive football coach) in discussion with the author, November 22, 2019.

128

rallied around the family of their young coach, the future legend Rick Pitino, who lost a newborn child early in the season.

So there is precedent for teams coming together after tragedy, but in Bainbridge, it was different. This was a high school in a small town, without the massive budgets that the college and pro teams often take for granted. They and their families lived and worked and dined and prayed and fellowshipped and grieved and hung out and played with the rest of the town.

Kirby Smart contacted Coach Littleton again, as he often did, this time asking what he could do to help honor his hometown's champions. The result was a celebration of the team by the Touchdown Club with a special guest speaker: Coach Kirby Smart.

"I'll be honest, I get asked to speak a lot, but I asked to speak at this event," Coach Smart explained to the capacity crowd. "You got me. You've been asking, but you got me now, because you put Bainbridge back on the map, put it where it's supposed to be."[140]

"He was a great speaker, of course, and he talked about what Bainbridge meant to him and he named people who had influenced him," recalled Littleton.

The event was limited to 275 people, and the tickets were all spoken for in less than two weeks.[141]

"I've never seen him look more relaxed and comfortable than when he was mingling with old classmates, coaches and the adults that raised him," added Powell Cobb. Having grown up in Athens, Cobb knows a little bit about Georgia football. He lived in Athens for 16 years and never missed a home game. The Dawgs, along with the miraculous 1991 Atlanta Braves, taught him from an early age that sports writing includes much more than telling what happened on the field or court. That was one reason why Kirby's visit to his home-

140 Cobb, Powell, "Georgia coach Kirby Smart reunites, gives inspirational message at packed out fundraiser," The Post Searchlight, May 17, 2019. https://www.thepostsearchlight.com/2019/05/17/georgia-coach-kirby-smart-reunites-gives-inspirational-message-at-packed-out-fundraiser/. Retrieved September 27, 2019.
141 Mark and Connie Mitchell (Bainbridge Touchdown Club leaders) in discussion with the author, December 16, 2019.

The state championship was truly a family event, with each member of the Littleton family contributing and sacrificing during the storm-ravaged season. Coach Jeff Littleton and wife, Kristi, celebrate with their daughters Anna Kate, who is a cheerleader and soccer player for Bainbridge High School, and Emily, who is a cheerleader for Bainbridge Middle School.

Georgia's coach is a great thing, the weekly texts from Smart to Littleton reveal something deeper. He might not live there anymore, but Bainbridge was still his team. The championship was his victory too, just as it also belonged to those living in Bainbridge and those who once lived there. That's what a community truly is.

Coach Kirby Smart's return to Bainbridge was one of the biggest local stories in the months after the championship. Of course one story continued to linger; the effects of Hurricane Michael were still being felt and calculated. Georgia Public Broadcasting produced a story on the one-year anniversary of the hurricane, and the results of the recovery were mixed. The amount of agricultural losses had climbed to 2.5 billion. The State of Georgia acted quickly with both relief and tax credits, but the federal government was extremely slow. According to the article, federal aid had only become available a few weeks before the first anniversary on October 10, 2019. A number of local farmers, it explained, were facing the real possibility of foreclosure.

Ringing the bell of victory

People celebrate victories in many different ways. Some raise the trophy high in the air, while others wave a flag bearing the team's logo in front of screaming fans. Michael Jordan famously wept as he held the Larry O'Brien trophy for the NBA championship just won by his 1991 Chicago Bulls.

On Channel 10's *Sports Talk* with Theo Dorsey, the host asked Bainbridge stars Randy Fillingame and Bowen Dodson what they did to celebrate when they returned home from Atlanta. Dodson went hunting early the next morning, and Fillingame celebrated with family. The ways to celebrate were seemingly endless.

And then there's ringing the bell.

In a sea of good news, another reason for gratitude came on the medical front, during 2019, for the father of Bainbridge players Michael and Andrew Ryan. Jeremy Ryan became eligible to ring the bell. For anyone who has dealt with chemotherapy or radiation treatments, ringing the bell is done at the end of the last treatment. Ryan reflected on his own battle with cancer and the journey of his kids and their teammates. "I'm a believer. I don't believe that God causes bad things like the hurricane, but I do believe He used them to challenge and inspire people," he explained. Jeremy Ryan wasn't allowed to attend the Bainbridge games because chemo and radiation patients are susceptible to catching illnesses, but he was able to catch them all on television, or online. He went to the championship game anyway. "I wasn't going to miss that."

So the recovery continued. People worked to rebuild and repair their homes and circumstances. People moved on with their lives, as people inevitably do after difficult times.

Even afterward, remnants of the massive storm remain visible. Some empty buildings, and even areas of debris are real and present reminders of Hurricane Michael.

There are other reminders of the fall of 2018 as well. In homes, cafes, and many businesses throughout Bainbridge, a souvenir of that period of history has become commonplace.

131

"Our front page from the state title game is hanging in countless businesses around town," explained Powell Cobb. "The Bainbridge community has fully embraced the 2018 team. They've reached a sort of 'Folk Hero' status, not just in Bainbridge but around Georgia as a whole, especially considering how nobody expected them to do what they did after Hurricane Michael."[142]

The parade, the Kirby Smart event, and the entire journey inspired Rev. Brooks, who also serves with the Fellowship of Christian Athletes, to make a remark to the F.C.A.'s area director in Thomasville. "Someone needs to write a book about this amazing journey," he said. Many others, including Bryce Worthy, had been saying for months that the story should become a book.

After the victory parade, the town held a meet-and-greet style reception for the team. The players posed for photos with adoring fans, many of whom also wanted footballs or souvenirs autographed by these teenage sports celebrities. Who, they wondered, would ever have imagined this before Hurricane Michael when the team had lost four of its first six games?

But these guys had done the impossible, and it was a team victory. It was a state championship earned by the offense, the defense, the special teams, the coaches, the trainers, the cheerleaders, the band, the faculty, the student body, and the screaming fans from across a community that was fighting adversity just as these kids were.

So that's how it happened. A small town dared to dream big, and its people lived that dream together.

---

142 Powell Cobb (managing editor, *The Post Searchlight)* in discussion with the author, December 3, 2019.

Images

Georgia High School Association
AAAAA
FOOTBALL
STATE CHAMPION
2018

of the champions

The Bainbridge coaches celebrate their state championship victory.

Stats

Of
The
Champions

Games 15
Year 2018
Overall Record (10-5) Sub-Region Record (3-1)

Bainbridge	Season/Results	Opposition
35	Seminole County (B)	0
15	Cairo (B)	7
6	Lincoln (Tallahassee, FL.)	28
13	Brooks County(Quitman)	15
0	Crisp County(B)	23
14	Tift County (B)	31
27	Veterans (B)	14
0	Warner Robins(Warner Robins)	38
49	Harris Co.(B)	0
44	Thomas County(TCC Stadium)	11
	1st round State 5A Playoffs	
40	Jones County(B)	13
	2nd round State 5A Playoffs	
26	Wayne County (Jaycee Stadium)	19
	Quarterfinals State 5A Playoffs	
23	Buford (Tom Riden Stadium)	20
	Semifinals State 5A Playoffs	
20	Stockbridge (Stockbridge)	19
	5A State Championship	
47	Warner Robins (Mercedez .Benz)	41 (3 O.T.)

Bainbridge				Opposition		
	201		First Downs		173	
	33.2	124.9	Rushing Yards		32.9	107.2
		121.1	Passing Yards			128.9
	43.3	246.0	Total Yards		53.6	236.1
22.2	10.1	1.0	Passes A/C/I	20.7	10.0	1.1
	4.6	28.3	Punts-Avg.		4.9	33.8
	26	12	Fumbles-Lost		43	18
		27	Total Turnovers		34	
	38	-263	QB Sacks by		15	-101
	113	947	Penalty Yards		119	1007
60	186	32%	3rd Down Pct.	57	182	31%
12	32	38%	4th Down Pct.	11	24	46%
493	843	58%	Gain Ply/Total Ply	468	806	58%

Tackles		Total	Tackles		Tackles		Big
#	Player	TT	Solo	Assists	For Loss	FF	Plays
34	Randy Fillingame	**123**	87	36	31	4	0
22	Bryce. Worthy	**102**	69	33	16.5	5	0
30	Roman Harrison	**97**	79	18	32	0	0
26	Anthony Brooks	**85**	61	24	30	0	0
9	Coryn Burns	**38**	34	4	1	0	0
5	Caleb McDowell	**36**	34	2	1	2	0
45	Tahari Tate	**35**	28	7	10	3	0
3	Deyon Bouie	**31**	30	1	0	0	0
37	Eric Sanders, Jr.	**30**	24	6	9	1	0
35	Amari Peterson	**28**	15	13	4	1	0
17	Zion Bouie	**27**	24	3	2	0	0
23	Ralph Register	**24**	17	7	7.5	0	0
10	Jaheim Jenkins	**21**	21	0	1	0	0
24	Tim Allison	**20**	12	8	2	0	0
7	Aaron Spivie	**18**	16	2	2	0	0
21	Fred Thompson	**16**	15	1	1	1	0
19	Tevin McCray	**13**	8	5	2	0	0
36	Sam Boutwell	**6**	5	1	1	1	0
25	Caleb Lewis	**5**	5	0	0	0	0
47	Jashon Mitchell	**4**	3	1	1	0	0
16	J'von Lee	**3**	0	3	0	0	0
18	Adrian Cooper	**3**	0	3	0	0	0
94	Joe Parrych	**2**	2	0	1	0	0
13	Braxton Johnson	**2**	2	0	0	0	0
55	Jacob McLaughlin	**2**	2	0	0	0	0
1	Quayde Hawkins	**1**	1	0	0	0	0
76	Tim Anderson	**1**	1	0	0	0	0
6	Jaylan Peterson	**1**	1	0	0	0	0
8	Michael Ryan	**1**	1	0	0	0	0
49	Arkeavious Marshall	**1**	1	0	1	0	0
50	Vic Wimberly	**1**	1	0	0	0	0
80	Simpson Bowles	**1**	1	0	0	0	0
59	Ben Mitchell	**1**	1	0	0	0	0

Rushing

Name	Games	Carries	Gain	Loss	Net.	Avg.	Td's	Long	10 Yds +	Game Avg.
Caleb McDowell	14	185	1048	84	964	5.2	12	78td	29	68.9
Rashad Broadnax	14	173	737	69	668	3.9	4	34	19	47.7
Tevin McCray	14	46	248	20	228	5.0	2	35	8	16.3
Aaron Spivie	15	3	58	0	58	19.3	2	34td	2	3.9
Deyon Bouie	15	21	80	26	54	2.6	0	16	2	3.6
Roman Harrison	15	2	23	0	23	11.5	0	23	1	1.5
Zion Bouie	13	4	22	0	22	5.5	0	9	0	1.7
Caleb Lewis	14	6	11	2	9	1.5	0	5	0	0.6
Jaylen Peterson	14	1	3	0	3	3.0	0	3	0	0.2
Latraveon Colbert	3	4	2	3	-1	-0.3	0	1	0	-0.3
Kendall Glover	3	1	0	13	-13	-13.0	0	-13	0	-4.3
Jackson Wheeler	15	1	0	14	-14	-14.0	0	-14	0	-0.9
Quyade Hawkins	15	46	82	115	-33	-0.7	5	13	2	-2.2
Caleb Harris	15	1	0	12	-12	-12.0	0	-7	0	-0.8
Center Snap	15	4	0	82	-82	-20.5	0	-7	0	-5.5
Team	15	12	0	25	-25	-2.1	0	-1	0	-1.7
Team	15	498	2314	440	1874	3.8	25	78td	63	**124.9**
Opposition	15	493	2206	598	1608	3.3	16	93td	47	**107.2**

Passing

Name	Games	Att.	Comp.	Yards	Td's	Int.	Long	CM Pct.	Yards Per Att.	Pass Rating	YDS Game
Quyade Hawkins	15	305	144	1695	12	14	61td	.472	5.56	97.7	**113.0**
Caleb Mcdowell	14	2	2	72	1	0	48	1.000	36.00	567.4	**5.1**
Deyon Bouie	15	15	4	38	0	0	19	.267	2.53	47.9	**2.5**
Jackson Wheeler	15	11	2	11	0	1	8	.182	1.00	8.4	**0.7**
Team	15	333	152	1816	13	15	61td	.456	5.45	95.3	**121.1**

#	Player	Games	Rec.	Yards	Avg.	Td's	Long
7	Aaron Spivie	15	44	555	12.6	3	48
22	Adrian Cooper	14	32	457	14.3	4	61td
6	Jaylen Peterson	14	17	150	8.8	1	23
8	Michael Ryan	15	12	132	11.0	0	31
5	Caleb McDowell	14	12	81	6.8	1	20
4	Rashad Broadnax	14	11	76	6.9	2	45td
3	Deyon Bouie	15	9	210	23.3	1	42
13	Braxton Johnson	13	5	76	15.2	0	24
22	Bryce Worthy	15	2	24	12.0	1	24td
44	Bowen Dodson	15	2	16	8.0	0	10
16	J'von Lee	15	2	7	3.5	0	4
49	Arkevious Marshall	12	1	14	14.0	0	14
14	Jackson Wheeler	15	1	10	10.0	0	13
50	Vick Wimberly	15	1	6	6.0	0	10
19	Tevin McCray	15	1	6	6.0	0	6
	Team	15	152	1820	12.0	13	61td

Made in the USA
Columbia, SC
02 November 2021

48226224R10085